Fight Fat and Win
LIGHT MEALS
AND SNACKS

Elaine Moquette-Magee

M.P.H., R.D.

CHRONIMED
PUBLISHING

Library of Congress Cataloging-in-Publication Data

Moquette-Magee, Elaine, M.P.H., R.D.

Fight Fat and Win Light Meals and Snacks: Lower the Fat in Yc Favorite Snacks and Create Light Meals You'd Never Know We Healthy. / Elaine Moquette-Magee, M.P.H., R.D.

     p.   cm.

Includes index

ISBN 1-56561-076-8; $12.95

     1. Low-fat diet — Recipes

     I. Title

Edited by: Jeff Braun and Jolene Steffer
Cover Design: Terry Dugan Design
Production Artist: Janet Hogge
Art/Production Manager: Claire Lewis
Printed in the United States of America

Published by
Chronimed Publishing
P.O. Box 59032
Minneapolis, MN 55459-9686

10   9   8   7   6   5   4   3   2   1

Table of Contents

Introduction V

Why Eat Light? 1

Are We Eating Light Meals and Snacks?....................................21

Junk Food Has Given Snacking a Bad Name..............................33

Recipes

Light Snacks 51
Decadent Late-Night Snacks & Delectable Desserts........81
Light Breakfasts 101
Light Lunches 141
Delightfully Light Dinners.....................................171

Taking it a Week at a Time: Sample Menus 243

Index 259

III

Acknowledgments

I would first like to thank David Wexler of Chronimed Publishing for thinking of me when he had this book idea. I also thank Dr. John DeCastro, Ph.D., professor of psychology at Georgia State University, who was refreshingly approachable when I asked him a long list of questions for this book. John also analyzed survey data and helped with several graphs. It was a pleasure to work with him.

Introduction

This entire book is devoted to helping you eat small, frequent meals throughout the day and also eat light at night. But rearranging your calories into many smaller meals and eating a light dinner is harder than it sounds for people who have not eaten that way most of their lives.

Many of us eat large dinners because that's what we've always done. We eat only two or three times a day because that's the norm. Our schedules revolve around the concept of breaking to eat at certain times of day. But I'll tell you, you very quickly shift your view of eating when you have children. When caring for toddlers especially, you become an instant believer in the sanctity of snacking. Toddlers, because of their small stomach size but high energy and rapid growth rate, need to eat frequently. (When you are making your third peanut butter & jelly sandwich within an hour, it sometimes seems like they never really stop eating.)

Although our stomachs grow larger as we grow up, and our growth needs, at least vertically, reduce to nil, I don't think we should necessarily outgrow the way we ate as children (eating small, frequent meals throughout the day). As adults we need to listen to our bodies better. Instead of telling our bodies when and how much we are going to eat, we should let our bodies tell us when we need food. Let your natural hunger rhythms guide you.

For some, eating small, frequent meals throughout the day is the easier part—eating light at night is the real challenge. Why, eating a small dinner is practically un-patriotic! But don't worry, this book is loaded with meal and menu examples to help guide you and lots and lots of recipes to help get you started.

VI

Why Eat Light?

The opposite of eating "light" is eating heavy. But who wants to eat heavy? Heavy meals make you feel weighed down, which is exactly what happens. Meals large in size or heavy in fat remain in your stomach longer. In fact, if eaten alone, fat takes the longest to empty from the stomach. Next comes protein, followed by carbohydrates, which empty the fastest from the stomach.

The longer food stays in the stomach, the longer some of your blood is diverted to your stomach. More blood for the stomach means less blood (and less oxygen, glucose energy, and other nutrients) for the brain and working muscles.

There are quite a few negative side effects associated with heavy eating (eating large, high-fat meals). The following list covers just a few of the symptoms, all of which spell discomfort with a capital "D."

Symptoms of Heavy Eating

- tiredness, lethargy;
- stomach pain or stomach ache;
- heartburn for some people;
- inability to exercise or move quickly for a long time after the meal (instead of light on your feet, you're not on your feet at all—you're laying on a couch, feet up);
- indigestion following some meals;
- unproductive at work or at home due to lethargy and stomach discomfort;
- loosening your belt to try to ease discomfort;
- and possibly, poor sleep due to one or more of the above.

What Is "Light" Eating?

According to nutrition labeling laws, "light" foods must have at least one-third fewer calories or one-half the fat grams when compared to the regular product. (Light can also be used to refer to the texture and color of a food; however, the label is supposed to spell this out—for example, light brown sugar.)

So "Why eat light?" is really two questions. First, "Why eat less fat?" and second, "Why eat smaller, more frequent meals?"

Why Eat Less Fat?

I have written entire books that examine the many health benefits of eating a diet low in fat. In a nutshell, a low-fat diet, rich in fiber, fruits, and vegetables, is the best way to help prevent cancer, heart disease, and obesity through diet.

2

People gravitate toward low-fat eating for all different reasons. Some because somebody close to them died at an early age from cancer or heart disease. For many it's the threat of a larger dress or pants size that keeps them counting fat grams.

If you want to eat fewer calories at dinner, then eating a low-fat dinner is a must. You see, a gram of fat contains more than twice the calories of a gram of carbohydrate or protein. So cut down on the fat and you will most likely see big calorie savings.

Eating less fat isn't only about looking good, although admittedly that's a powerful motivator—it's about feeling good and living longer.

Why Not Eat Less Fat?

If low-fat eating can be made painless; if you can eat less fat and still have your favorite foods and flavors too; and if you can prepare healthy meals without spending additional time in the kitchen, then the pertinent question should be, "Why NOT eat less fat?"

While writing this book, my neighbor told me about her cousin who died suddenly of a heart attack at the age of 52. The cousin was a pediatrician who reveled in his daily rituals of high-cholesterol, high-fat meals and six packs of Coke. He considered himself completely immune to the threats of heart disease. After all, his genes were good, his mom and dad were still alive and kicking in their 80s, and his blood cholesterol was only 120. He boasted that he could eat anything he wanted. But what he may have chosen to ignore is the fact that high blood cholesterol is only one of many risk factors for heart disease (some of which are not yet known). It's been reported that half of all heart attack victims don't even have high blood cholesterol.

There is no guarantee that eating a low-fat diet will protect you from

The calories you eat during the day are likely to go for fuel (energy burned during awake hours), while the calories you eat at night are more likely to go to storage (body fat and a small amount of carbohydrate stored as glycogen).

3

early death from cancer or heart disease. But it should help stack the deck in your favor. If you can eat low fat without giving up flavor, favorite foods, and convenience, then there is no reason not to eat low-fat meals and snacks.

The Health Benefits of Grazing

Think about when your body needs energy the most. It makes sense for your meals to match your metabolic needs. Depending on the exact composition and size of your meal, your blood glucose (blood sugar) begins to rise 30 to 60 minutes after eating and peaks about 1 1/2 to 2 hours after the meal. This is when you have the highest supply of immediate energy. So what you eat for breakfast is your fuel for what's ahead for the morning. What you eat for lunch is your fuel for the afternoon. And what you eat for dinner fuels your late-evening activities and sleep.

There are at least seven good reasons to eat small, frequent meals throughout the day.

1. Your brain and body require a constant supply of energy in the blood. Eating small, frequent meals throughout the day is more likely to keep your blood sugar (and energy) stable. Because your body constantly uses energy, you should give it constant energy. Obviously we can't nibble all day long. But eating small, frequent meals throughout the day gets the job done better than two large meals.

2. When you eat small, frequent meals, you are more likely to prevent low blood sugar levels, which can trigger headaches, irritability, food cravings, or overeating episodes in susceptible people.

3. Eating small, frequent meals encourages weight loss or weight maintenance because you are less likely to overeat at any meal (particularly if you eat when you're hungry and stop when you're comfortably full). If you flood your bloodstream with a load of fat, protein, and carbohydrate calories from a large meal, your body has to get rid of any extra calories. Fats can be deposited in fat storage cells; carbohydrates can be converted to their storage form (glycogen) or converted to fat storage; and extra protein not used for muscle maintenance or synthesizing enzymes and hormones can eventually be converted to fat.

4. Women may be able to alleviate some of the symptoms of PMS and menopause by keeping blood sugar levels fairly stable. (These are times when your body is even more sensitive to changes in blood sugar levels.)

5. By eating small, frequent meals (especially ones low in fat) you may also avoid quick rises of serum triglycerides, another type of blood fat.

6. By eating more often, you increase the amount of calories you burn digesting, absorbing, and metabolizing food. That's right, the body burns calories when it digests and absorbs food. And every time we eat, the digestion process kicks into gear. So, by spreading the same amount of food over two or three small meals instead of one big meal, we start the digestive process two or three times instead of just once; therefore burning more calories. And we're not just talking about a few calories burned here and there either. This increase in metabolism that occurs during the digestion, absorption, and metabolism of carbohydrates, fat, and protein called the thermic effect of food burns 5 to 10 percent of the total calories we consume!

7. It's physically more comfortable to eat small, frequent meals. A huge meal takes longer to empty entirely from the stomach than a small one. When you eat light, you're not weighed down by a large meal in your stomach. You might feel like you have more energy because a substantial portion of your blood isn't being diverted to the stomach to help digest a large meal. And since fat slows down the rate at which the food in the stomach is released into the small intestine, the more fat in a large meal, the longer that blood is diverted.

The Health Benefits of Eating Light at Night

We burn about 70 percent of our calories as fuel during the daytime hours. But when do many of us eat the majority of our calories? During the evening hours. Your body metabolizes those calories when you are expending the least amount of energy (burning the fewest calories). It doesn't make metabolic sense, does it?

Eating the majority of your calories at night can take its toll on your health and your waistline. In a recent study, people were given one 2,000-calorie meal per day, either in the morning or the evening. All the people in the breakfast group lost weight, while four of the six people in the evening group gained weight.

There are at least two reasons to eat light at night.

1. The calories from your dinner meal and thereafter basically supply your body with energy for your night's sleep and possibly the first couple hours of morning. Your body simply doesn't need many calories while it sleeps—no matter how restless your sleep is.

6

2. If you overeat, especially during the evening hours, the extra calories (calories in excess of your energy needs) will likely be converted to stored energy—primarily as fat.

Timing is Everything

Computing how many calories are needed or burned is not an exact science. There are many individual components that affect the numbers. For example, three things to factor into the eating light at night equation are: "When is dinner eaten?" "When is bedtime?" and "Is there any physical activity in the evening?"

There can be a big difference between eating dinner at 6 o'clock or eating dinner at 8 o'clock when your bedtime is at 10. The earlier your dinner the more likely you will use some of those calories before bedtime. In other words, the later your dinner, the more important it is that you eat light at night.

Exercise is great any time of day—whenever you can fit it into your schedule—but here is one advantage to working out in the evening: Calories burned in the evening will increase substantially if one of your evening activities is an hour-long exercise class or 30 minutes on a treadmill or rowing machine. Not only do you burn calories while exercising, but your metabolism tends to remain higher than normal for several hours after a workout.

Working out at night may have an added bonus, too. For some people, vigorous exercise can help suppress the appetite (by experience, though, I would exclude swimming from this group). So it is possible you will be more likely to eat light at night if your early evening plans include some form of exercise. Even taking a walk after dinner will help increase the calories you burn and it may help you refrain from late-night snacking.

Dinner: The Least Important Meal of the Day?

How could dinner be the least important meal? This is the meal where families come together, where we sit down in the company of friends and family and enjoy a nice, relaxing meal. This is the meal that celebrates the end of a workday or the pleasures of a weekend. All this being true, dinner is important socially, not physiologically.

By evening, physiologically your body is gearing down for the sleep zone. It is spending fewer calories to function than it did earlier that day. By the time your dinner is digested and the energy starts entering the blood system, you may be crawling into bed for a long winter's nap. So eating after dinner (unless you are truly hungry) is a nutritional "no-no." When you consume excess calories late at night, you are essentially feeding your fat cells.

How many calories do we normally burn, beyond our normal metabolism, after work and during the evening? Well, let's say we drive home for about 30 minutes (that's 30 calories). Then maybe we fold laundry for half an hour (that's 45 more calories) and watch television for an hour while paying bills (that's 28 calories). While sleeping, we burn zero additional calories beyond our basal metabolism. That's a total of 103 extra calories burned. Get the picture? If you exercise during the evening, of course, you will add many more calories to this total.

Five Steps to Eating Light at Night

Eating light at night goes against our upbringing. Large (often high-fat) dinners are woven tightly into American culture. But should we trade our pot roast dinners for pumpkin puree or our lasagna for salad? Not at all. Take it step by step.

The first step is to serve low-fat dinners and desserts as often as possible. Fat has more than twice the calories (per gram) of protein or carbohydrate. So if eating fewer calories at night is the goal, eating low-fat dinners is a good first step.

The second step is to serve small to moderate portions at dinner and dessert. Everyone should eat until they are comfortably full, so if someone needs another helping, they should feel free to help themselves. But generally, if you eat small, frequent meals and snacks throughout the day (eating when hungry), you will be satisfied with a moderate portion.

The third step is to select food choices for dinner that lend themselves to lightness, like all-in-one dishes, hearty soups, dinner salads, etc.

The fourth step is to educate your family on the health virtues of eating light at night so they'll be more willing to try it. Hopefully after a few days or weeks, they'll notice how much better they feel.

The fifth and final step is to discourage late-night eating and big desserts—since late-night snacking is the most popular time to snack in America. (As if we don't eat enough calories during dinner!)

Breaking the Fast With Breakfast

I usually wake up ready to dive face first into a bowl of anything that doesn't move. Why? Because I've made it a habit to eat light at night. I find it restful to go to sleep without a full stomach and invigorating to wake up ravenous. The lighter your dinner, the more important breakfast becomes—and that's good. Breakfast should be important. It helps to fuel our morning and possibly early afternoon activities. But guess what? Breakfast is the meal most often skipped by Americans age 8 and over, according to a survey conducted by the National Restaurant Association in 1991. And skipping breakfast is on the rise. Ten years earlier we skipped, on average, 1.4 breakfasts a week compared to 1.6 in 1991. The next meal most often skipped is lunch.

I must mention, however, that individuals have their own unique eating patterns. Many people just aren't all that hungry first thing in the morning. So pack a substantial morning snack for when the hunger does kick in.

Lunch: The Most Important Meal of the Day

Lunch. It's not the first meal and it's not the last, but metabolically speaking it's probably the most important one. When you eat a meal, it's really a caloric investment for the future. (Your body probably won't have access to the majority of those calories for an hour or more.) Since most of us aren't very active at night, that rules out dinner as the most important meal of the day, leaving breakfast and lunch. Breakfast is an important meal—don't get me wrong—but lunch is probably more important.

Surveys show that, for most of us, the largest meal of the day tends to be dinner and the most popular time to snack is in the evening. If you skip lunch or eat a practically nonexistent one, you might feel irritable or fatigued by afternoon. And you'll be more likely to overeat during and after dinner because your blood sugar dropped below comfortable levels. Most of us have enough carbohydrate stores (glycogen) to fuel us through the morning should we have to miss breakfast. But many of us treat lunch as an expendable luxury—we have a nice, relaxing lunch only if we have time for it.

Maybe this has happened to you: You are busy at work or running errands all day long with no time to stop for lunch or a quick snack. Finally you arrive home, tired and ravenous. You start picking through the kitchen cabinets, going through the refrigerator, snacking on just about anything you can find. Finally, about 40 minutes later, you"ve "snacked" on 1,000 calories or more. What happened? You pushed your body past the comfortable hunger point and now your body is trying to make up for all the meals or snacks you missed during the day.

Back to Calories In and Calories Out

With all the talk about fat grams and fat-free products, some of us have lost sight of one important concept—calories in and calories out. When "calories in" is equal to "calories out," theoretically, weight (and body fat) should be stable. If "calories in" is more than "calories out" (your body's energy needs), the extra calories, especially fat calories, are most likely stored in fat cells. It's true that when you are at rest your body uses carbohydrate and fat simultaneously to produce energy. But once that extra energy is stored as fat in certain places like the belly, buttocks, hips, thighs, etc. (particularly for women), your body tends to hold on to it for dear life—trust me on that one.

We're more likely to eat only what our body needs if we space our food throughout the day, avoiding extreme hunger or long gaps between meals, and avoiding overeating at meals.

Loosening the Basic 4

Eating five small meals a day may require splitting up the Basic 4 Food Groups. You don't have to have all 4 food groups represented in every meal. When you eat five small meals, there is plenty of room to fit them all in. Here's an example of how the servings may be spread out through the day:

Breakfast—1/2 - 1 cup fruit, 2 grain servings

Examples:

Oatmeal with raisins, orange juice

Toast with low-sugar fruit spread or diet margarine

Melon cubes

Morning Snack—1 milk group serving, 1 grain serving

Examples:

Low-fat crackers with reduced-fat cheese

Low-fat yogurt with low-fat granola cereal

Lunch—1/2 - 1 cup vegetables (or 2 cups dark green lettuce), 1 meat group serving, 2 grain servings

Examples:

Tuna salad sandwich with vegetable sticks

Spaghetti made with lean meat and vegetables

Afternoon Snack—1/2 - 1 cup of fruit, 1 milk group serving

Examples:

A handful of dried fruit and a glass of low-fat milk

Apple wedges and reduced-fat cheese

13

Dinner—1 cup vegetables (or 2 cups dark green lettuce), 1 meat group serving, 2 grain servings

Examples:

Grilled fish and vegetables over rice

Ground sirloin hamburger on bun with low-fat french
  fries (3 or less grams of fat per serving) and large
  green salad

Number of Servings for Each Food Group

Fruit & Vegetables Group = 5 to 8 servings

Grain Group = 7 to 8 servings

Milk Group = 2 to 3 servings

Meat Group = 2 servings

What's the Right Size Meal for You?

You should eat enough—but not too much. Can I be any more vague? But truly, there is no magic number of calories to recite. No secret equation to explain. It depends on your calorie expenditure, which depends on your physical activity, your body size, and your metabolism, just to name a few factors.

Eating small, frequent meals and eating light at night for someone who normally eats 2,000 calories might look like this:

500 calories	breakfast
600 calories	lunch
400 calories	dinner

Plus: 2 snacks worth about 250 calories each

Or:

400 calories	small meal 1
400 calories	small meal 2
400 calories	small meal 3
400 calories	small meal 4
400 calories	small meal 5

14

For someone with a larger calorie expenditure, like 2,700 calories, it might look more like this:

700 calories	breakfast
800 calories	lunch
600 calories	dinner

Plus: 2 snacks worth about 300 calories each

Or:

540 calories	small meal 1
540 calories	small meal 2
540 calories	small meal 3
540 calories	small meal 4
540 calories	small meal 5

I'm not suggesting you count calories or grams of fat on a regular basis; I don't believe in it. I think it makes people obsessed with food, and that's counterproductive to health. The sample meals that follow will give you an idea of what a moderately sized meal feels like in your stomach without having to resort to counting calories. You'll find more sample menus starting on page 243.

15

Sample Meal Sizes

It's difficult to visualize what all these numbers mean spread out over a day. So take a look at some of the sample meals below and notice their size and estimated calories.

500-Calorie Morning Meal

Scrambled eggs (made with 1 egg beaten with 1/4 cup fat-free egg substitute and cooked in a nonstick pan coated with nonstick cooking spray)

2 slices whole wheat toast (one piece of toast spread with 1 tsp diet margarine and the other spread with 2 tsp of jam)

8 oz orange juice

Total—Calories 433, fat 11 gm (23% calories from fat)

Bagel & cream cheese (spread with 2 Tbsp light cream cheese)

2 slices less-fat turkey bacon (e.g., Louis Rich) cooked till crisp

8 oz orange juice

Total—Calories 412, fat 11.5 gm (25% calories from fat)

1 1/2 cups Raisin Bran cereal with

3/4 cup 1% low-fat milk, and

1/2 cup sliced strawberries

8 oz orange juice

Total—Calories 467, fat 4 gm (8% calories from fat)

750-Calorie Morning Meal

Light egg muffin sandwich (made with 1 toasted English muffin, 1 piece lean ham, 1 oz reduced-fat cheese, and 1/4 cup fat-free egg substitute fried in 2 tsp diet margarine or 1 tsp regular butter or margarine)

1 1/2 cups cornflakes with

3/4 cup low-fat milk, and

1/2 cup fresh or frozen raspberries

Total—Calories 700, fat 17.5 gm (23% calories from fat)

2 pieces low-fat coffee cake

1 cup fresh fruit salad dressed with

1/2 cup flavored low-fat yogurt

1 cup 2% low-fat milk

Total—Calories 764, fat 18 gm (21% calories from fat)

Oatmeal (made with 3/4 cup dry oats cooked with 1 1/3 cup low-fat milk) with

1/8 cup raisins and 2 Tbsp maple syrup stirred into cooked oatmeal

2 slices less-fat turkey bacon (e.g., Louis Rich) cooked till crisp

8 oz orange juice

Total—Calories 716, fat 15.6 gm (20% calories from fat)

700-Calorie Mid-Day Meal

Grilled cheese sandwich (made with 2 slices bread, 1 1/2 oz reduced-fat cheese [5 gm fat per oz], and 1 1/2 tsp diet margarine spread on outside of bread)

1 apple

2 oz pretzels

Total—Calories 679, fat 16 gm (21% calories from fat)

2 large slices thick crust cheese pizza (1/8 of large Round Table restaurant pizza used for analysis)

Green salad (2 cups looseleaf lettuce, 2-3 cherry tomatoes, 1/4 cup kidney beans, sliced cucumber, and 3 Tbsp low-calorie Italian dressing)

10 oz lemonade

Total—Calories 669, fat 19.5 gm (26% calories from fat)

Turkey deli sandwich (made with submarine roll, 4 oz roasted turkey breast, sliced tomato, lettuce, and 1 Tbsp low-fat mayonnaise)

1 cup fresh fruit salad

Total—Calories 694, fat 12 gm (16% calories from fat)

1,050-Calorie Mid-Day Meal

3 large slices thick crust cheese pizza (1/8 of large Round Table restaurant pizza used for analysis)

Green salad (2 cups looseleaf lettuce, 2-3 cherry tomatoes, 1/4 cup kidney beans, sliced cucumber, and 3 Tbsp low-calorie Italian dressing)

18

10 oz lemonade
3 Fig newton cookies

Total—Calories 1,050, fat 30.6 gm (26% calories from fat)

450-Calorie Evening Meal

Spaghetti (made with 1 cup cooked noodles, 1/2 cup spaghetti sauce, and 2 oz cooked ground sirloin)

1 cup steamed broccoli

Total—Calories 444, fat 11 gm (21% calories from fat)

Teriyaki chicken (1 skinless chicken breast cooked with 1/4 cup teriyaki sauce) served with

3/4 cup steamed rice, and

1 cup cooked carrots

Total—Calories 470, fat 4 gm (7% calories from fat)

19

Hamburger (includes 3 oz cooked ground sirloin, catsup, and bun)

1 cup oven french fries (e.g., Ore Ida potato wedges)

Carrot and celery sticks (1 carrot and 1 celery stalk, cut into sticks)

Total—Calories 479, fat 12 gm (23% calories from fat)

Burying any Barriers to Eating Small, Frequent Meals

As I see it, there are basically three barriers to eating small, frequent meals throughout the day and eating light at night.

Barrier 1

Family traditions and expectations reinforce large dinners. And, it's an all-too-common habit to follow a large dinner with a big dessert. But family style dinners aren't the problem—it's the size of the dinner and amount of fat in the dinner that are the problems.

Barrier 2

Work schedules usually don't encourage eating many small meals throughout the day. Everything focuses on the lunch or dinner hour. So, some people simply take a break when they can and eat a large lunch or wait until they get home and eat a large dinner. But these people shouldn't be surprised when they fall asleep at their desk or in front of the TV because their large lunch or dinner has decreased their energy and made them uncomfortable.

Barrier 3

It's not socially acceptable to eat small, frequent meals—yet.

I'm not going to sugarcoat it; it ain't going to be easy knocking these barriers down. But the health benefits are great and the rewards of feeling better and having more energy are almost immediate. So don't let all these people and traditions hold you back. Go forth and eat small, frequent meals throughout the day and eat light at night. Set an example for your family (barrier #1), for your workplace (barrier #2), heck—for the entire country (barrier #3).

Are We Eating Light Meals and Snacks?

Trying to write this chapter was like trying to find fruit at a fast food restaurant. I wanted to get a general picture of our calorie needs versus actual intake throughout the day, particularly in the evening. I ran into one problem, though. Estimates of how many calories the average male or female burns after dinner and until morning are not easily available. Not many researchers want to attach a number, or even a range of numbers, to this question due to the differences between individuals. But I found one researcher that would.

Dr. Gail Butterfield, Ph.D., a metabolic researcher in California, estimates your body burns between 700 and 1,100 calories after dinner until morning. Of course, the exact number of calories varies greatly depending on your sex, size, activity level, and personal metabolism—but this range is a good guesstimate.

Still, I needed to get a feel for how many calories we consume, on average, during dinner and in the evening. I wanted to see how this compares to the amount of calories we actually need. It seems clear that many people consume a whole lot more calories during and after dinner than they burn. But I wanted facts to back up this hunch.

Again, I ran into problems. This time, I looked for diet surveys that determined when calories are consumed during the day. Unfortunately, most diet surveys calculate the total amount of calories, fat, carbohydrates, etc., during the entire day.

However, I did find a researcher who had recent diet data that we could analyze—determining when people ate their calories and fat. I also hoped to shed light on several other interesting questions like whether people who eat small, frequent meals through the day tend to eat more or fewer total calories or grams of fat for the entire day. Incidentally, this researcher, John DeCastro, Ph.D., professor of psychology at Georgia State University, is one of few researchers to publish anything on meal sizes, patterns, and related factors.

Dr. DeCastro's studies suggest several things about eating at the end of day versus the beginning or middle:

1. Evening food intake is relatively high in fat compared to earlier meals.

2. Meal size tends to increase over the day with peaks at lunch and dinner.

3. Meal fullness/satisfaction (the satiety ratio) declines late in the day, which suggests that eating at this time is less satisfying.

4. The longer the gap between the previous meal or snack and dinner, the larger dinner tends to be. Interestingly, the gap between eating is a significant predictor of meal size for dinner only.
(#1-4 were all presented in Physiology & Behavior, *Vol. 40 pp. 437-446, 1987)*

5. Meals eaten with other people are an average of 44 percent larger than meals eaten alone, and include larger amounts of carbohydrates, fat, protein, and alcohol. In fact, the more people present, the larger the meal tends to be. *(Physiology & Behavior, Vol. 51, pp. 121-125, 1992)*

And the Survey Says . . .

For more than 10 years, Dr. DeCastro and his colleagues have been collecting and analyzing the food diaries of about 750 people (326 men and 432 women). The participants' ages range from 18 to 85, with an average age of 38. Study participants record their food intake for seven days (thereby including weekdays and the weekend) and describe each meal or snack, the time of day, and various emotional and environmental factors. The results are then analyzed by a software program written by Dr. DeCastro and based on a proprietary data base developed by Nutran Inc.

A word of caution: The information described here demonstrates how specific meal and snack sizes and other factors may be associated with certain findings. But we cannot say they are the unequivocal cause. To establish a direct relationship between meal and snack intakes and overall daily intakes we would have to control virtually every activity of a study group.

It is difficult when interpreting Dr. DeCastro's findings to know what comes first—something like the chicken or the egg dilemma. For instance, do people who eat small, frequent meals tend to eat fewer calories and fat grams because they tend to be more health conscious in general? Or is it partly due to the food choices or something innate in that particular meal pattern? It's hard to tell. But the results are certainly interesting and offer insight into the very complex issue of what, when, how, and why we eat.

23

Do people who eat large, infrequent meals during the day eat more calories or fat grams than people who eat small, frequent meals?

Eating small, frequent meals was indeed associated with a lower overall intake of calories and grams of fat compared to people who ate large, infrequent meals, according to the data. In fact, people who ate small, frequent meals consumed, on average, 8 percent fewer calories per day, 22 percent less fat, and 8 percent less protein than their counterparts. They also ate more carbohydrates.

Incidentally, for men, small, frequent meals were defined as more than 4.01 meals per day with fewer than 567 calories at each meal. For women, it was 3.9 meals per day with fewer than 423 calories at each meal.

Large, infrequent meals for men were defined as fewer than 3.22 meals per day with more than 734 calories at each meal. For women, it was 3.15 meals per day with more than 541 calories at each meal.

24

Men	Small, Frequent Meals	Large, Infrequent Meals
Total Calories	2,196	2,382
% Calories From Fat	33%	39%
Grams of Fat	81 gm	103 gm
% Calories From Protein	15%	17%
% Calories From Carbohydrate	51%	41%

Women	Small, Frequent Meals	Large, Infrequent Meals
Total Calories	1592	1717
% Calories From Fat	33%	39%
Grams of Fat	57.5 gm	74 gm
% Calories From Protein	17%	16%
% Calories From Carbohydrate	50%	42%

Do people who eat light at night eat fewer calories and grams of fat overall than people who eat larger dinners and nighttime snacks?

Yes, those who had a light snack at night ate 9.3 percent fewer total calories and 10 percent less fat overall compared to those who ate larger nighttime snacks. However, eating light at dinner was associated with eating 7.7 percent more total calories and 9.5 percent more fat than eating a larger amount at dinner. This shows the importance of knowing the benefits of light snacking because it appears many of the eaters of light dinners became not-so-light snackers at night.

Eating a light breakfast also seems to lead to eating more calories and fat throughout the day. A light breakfast was associated with eating 5.4 percent more total daily calories and 16.5 percent more fat grams than eating a larger amount at breakfast.

As for lunch and morning and afternoon snacks, eating large or small amounts made no difference in the overall average amount of calories eaten in the day.

25

What I find most interesting are the impressive results for the first and last times we eat each day; a light breakfast is associated with a higher overall intake of calories and fat while a light evening snack is associated with a lower overall intake of calories and fat.

How do we distribute our daily calories?

The following graph shows how study participants distributed their total calories across the six meal and snack periods. As a group, 41.8 percent of their total calories were eaten during and after dinner, but only 21.5 percent of their total calories were eaten during the breakfast and morning snack period.

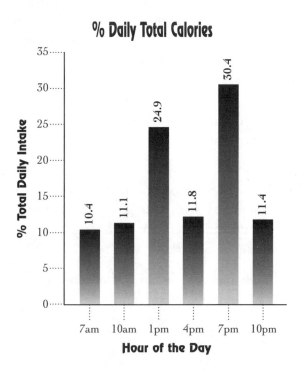

How do we distribute our total fat grams?

I was most excited about seeing the answer to this question. The following graph shows that, on average, breakfast tends to be our lowest-fat meal of the day. Even adding the fat from the breakfast and morning snack periods totals 19 percent of the total fat compared to 26.8 percent for the lunch period and 31 percent for the dinner period only.

We've already discussed the possible benefits of eating light at night—particularly light in fat. (By the time nighttime calories are digested and absorbed, we are most likely sleeping and our body is most likely in a "storage" mode rather than an "energy burning" mode.) Well, for these study participants, 42 percent of their total fat intake was consumed during dinner and the nighttime snack period.

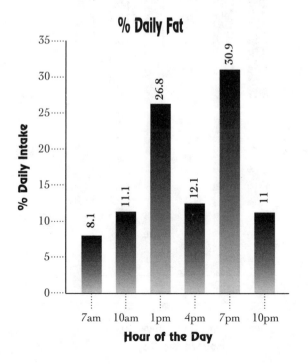

% Daily Fat

Dr. DeCastro analyzed how the percent of daily calories from carbohydrate, protein, and fat changed during the day. (See the following graph.) He found the proportion of calories from carbohydrates tended to decline as the day went on, while the proportion of calories from fat and protein tended to increase, particularly for meals (as compared to snacks).

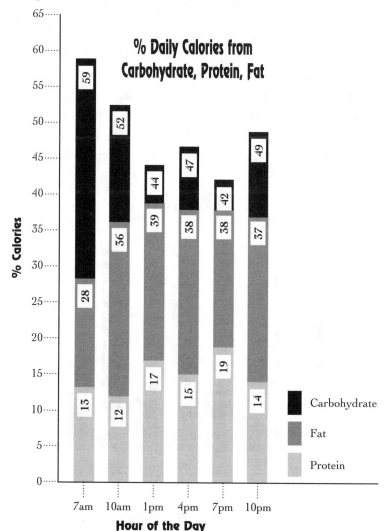

% Daily Calories from Carbohydrate, Protein, Fat

Why do we eat so much in the evening?

There are probably many reasons why a large portion of our total calories is eaten during and after dinner, including physiological, emotional, and cultural influences. The following are some possible influences I came up with; you may have your own to add to the list.

— It's part of our culture to eat a large dinner. It's also customary in many homes to enjoy a large dessert after most dinners.

— With breakfast and lunch being catch as catch can, dinner may be the only social meal people have during the workday, and studies show people tend to eat more around others.

— Some people, especially women, skip meals or undereat during the day, possibly sending their body into a state of deprivation for which their body tries to make up at night. It can take quite a lot of food to satisfy the body's hunger from a day of undereating. You may recall that research has shown the time between the previous meal or snack and dinner is a predictor of dinner size. In other words, the longer the gap between a previous meal or snack and dinner, the larger the dinner.

— Overeating at dinner or late at night may calm people from hassles and stresses that build during the day.

— Some research suggests that eating later in the day may be less satisfying than eating the same amount of food earlier in the day. Perhaps we eat more food in the evening because it simply takes more food to satisfy us at that time of day.

— As mentioned earlier, studies show that meals eaten

29

with others are, on average, 44 percent larger than meals eaten alone. And since dinner tends to be the meal most likely shared with other people, this may partially explain why it's also most likely to be the largest meal.

Sensible Take-Home Suggestions

Here are seven sensible take-home suggestions based on the data analysis presented here and Dr. DeCastro's previous work:

1. Since evening meals and snacks tend to be the highest in fat, this is the time of day to try our hardest to make healthier choices.

2. Since meal size tends to increase over the day and peak at dinner, eating smaller evening meals might be our greatest challenge. We have to be careful of the popular nighttime snack period. For some people, a small dinner leads to a big late-night snack talespin—and that's not good. So, concentrate on eating a low-fat dinner and, if you get hungrier later, select a low-fat evening snack or dessert.

3. Since we often eat larger dinners when there's a long gap between lunch or snack and dinner, it might behoove us to eat lunch and an afternoon snack to help avoid overeating at dinner.

4. People who eat small, frequent meals tend to eat fewer total calories and fat grams than those who eat large, infrequent meals. It's difficult to know exactly what is at work here, but give it a go; see if eating small, frequent meals improves the way you eat and feel.

5. Eating a small breakfast is associated with eating more total fat at the end of the day. So, make sure you eat a substantial and satisfying breakfast that includes carbohydrates, protein, and some fat.

6. Eating a light nighttime snack is associated with eating fewer calories and less fat overall. So avoid large or high-fat evening snacks.

7. Forty-two percent of the participants' total calories were eaten during and after dinner, while only 21.5 percent of the total calories were eaten during the breakfast and morning snack period. So, most of us should shift some of our calories from the heavier dinner and after-dinner periods to the calorically light (but probably more important metabolically) breakfast and morning snack periods.

Junk Food Has Given Snacking a Bad Name

Snacking in and of itself isn't bad. It's what we snack *on* and *when* we snack that gets us into trouble. In fact, snacking can be a good thing. There are three keys to healthy snacking:

The Keys to Healthy Snacking

1. Eat light during your main meals: breakfast, lunch, and especially dinner

2. Try not to snack after dinner unless you are truly hungry

3. Select snack items that won't add excessive fat or sugar to your daily total

How do we rate against The Keys to Healthy Snacking? Let's start with Key #1. Many people eat large, high-fat meals, especially at dinner. If we eat large meals and then snack, we will most likely be overconsuming in the calorie and fat departments. The point, of course, is to eat light meals and snack a couple times a day to provide your body with an almost constant supply of food energy and eliminate long periods of no food and intense hunger. It also avoids overloading your body with an excess of calories all at once.

The flip side of that coin is to skip meals during important times of the day, like breakfast or lunch, which may encourage an overeating response during snacking or dinner. The survey, Meal Consumption Behavior—1991, by the National Restaurant Association reported that breakfast was the meal most often skipped by individuals eight years and older. Twenty-one percent of the men and 19 percent of the women said they skipped breakfast five or more times a week. Only 5.5 percent of the men and 5.1 of the women said they skipped lunch. And practically no one—less than 1 percent—skipped dinner.

As for Key #2, according to the *Good Housekeeping* survey, 1990 Food Trends, more Americans snack in the evening than any other time of the day—the worst possible time to snack. Of the 200 women surveyed, 176 said between-meal snacking is permitted in their homes. These women were then asked whether they and their families ate mid-morning snacks, afternoon snacks, and evening snacks. Fifty-five percent said their family snacked in the evening four or more times a week. Only 10 percent said they never ate evening snacks or ate them less than once a week. The next most popular time to snack is the afternoon. Forty-five percent said their family snacked in the afternoon four or more times a week. But 24 percent said they never ate afternoon snacks or ate them less than once a week. In last place was the mid-morning snack. Almost 18 percent said their family ate mid-morning snacks and another 8.5 percent said they ate them less than once a week.

To rate ourselves against Healthy Snacking Key #3, we need to know what Americans are snacking on.

In the *Good Housekeeping* survey, participants were asked which snacks their families ate regularly. They also asked women with children 5 years old or younger which snack foods their children requested. Women with children between the ages of 6 and 12 were asked the same questions. The top 20 snacks mentioned were pretty much the same in all three lists, but the order changed a bit. The one exception was nachos, which made the top 20 in every list except the one for children age 5 and under.

Top 20 Snacks

The information presented below was collected from 176 women surveyed who said between-meal snacking is permitted in their homes. These women were then asked which snacks they and their families ate regularly. There were obviously multiple answers, because rarely does a person or family snack on only one food.

Snack Foods	% of families that say they eat it regularly
Popcorn	65%
Fruit (fresh & canned)	63
Ice cream (premium & light)	52
Cookies	51
Chips/salty snacks	40
Potato chips	35
Crackers (alone)	34
Cheese (alone)	31
Crackers & cheese	31
Cereal	29
Yogurt/frozen bars	28
Candy/candy bars	24
Doritos	23
Popsicles/fruit bars	20.5
Leftovers	17
Nachos	16.5
Vegetables	16.5
Cake	16
Microwavable snacks/food	15
Peanut butter (alone)	12
Granola bars	12

What are we doing right?

First, let's look at the previous list with an optimistic eye, shall we? We are actually doing a few things right. The number one snack is popcorn. As long as one of the lower-fat, lower-sodium microwave popping corns are used, or it's a low-fat homemade popcorn recipe, popcorn is actually a pretty good snack choice. It's high in fiber and carbohydrate and contains other essential nutrients, and if it's low in fat, it has relatively few calories.

The number two snack is fruit and the number 17 snack is vegetables — I couldn't have thought of better snacks myself. Snacking on fruits and vegetables is a great way to reach the recommended daily goal of eating five servings of fruits and vegetables a day. Many of us focus on the grains, meats, and dairy groups during meals, making one-dish casseroles, sandwiches, tacos, etc., while neglecting the fruit and vegetable groups. One way to make sure you're getting them is to have them as snacks.

36

The 11th most common snack is yogurt. Most of the yogurts on the market are low in fat. Low-fat yogurt has many redeeming values, namely protein and other important nutrients found in dairy products. I prefer the taste of low-fat yogurt made with sugar, not Nutrasweet, as long as it isn't too sweet. You can tell which ones have the most sugar added by checking the nutrition label.

What can we do better?

You don't necessarily have to trade in your Chips Ahoy for a carrot stick, or your carton of ice cream for a carton of tofu to make better snack choices. You can have your chips and cookies and snack on them too — simply by making better choices in the supermarket. The following pages are full of information to help you choose the lower fat, lower sugar selections of many of the top 20 snack foods from the survey.

Popcorn (#1 Snack)

Whether you make yours fresh or pull puffed popcorn bags from the microwave, you control the amount of fat and calories in your popcorn. There are two ways fat is added to the perfectly wholesome, naturally low-fat popcorn kernel: Fat can be added when the kernel is being popped, usually in the form of oil. And it can be added for flavor after the kernel is popped, usually in the form of butter.

For lower-fat homemade popcorn, try using an air popper or one of the new microwave popping devices requiring no oil to pop the popcorn. Once the popcorn is popped, you can flavor your popcorn with Parmesan cheese, Italian herbs, garlic powder, cajun spice blends, etc. Some people also like using I Can't Believe It's Not Butter spray. But if you feel popcorn without butter isn't worth popping, try adding the least amount of butter you possibly can. Diet margarine isn't a good option here because its higher water content will make the popcorn soggy.

If microwave popping corn is your passion, you can find a light version in almost every brand on the market. My favorite is Orville Redenbacher light, butter flavor.

The cheese stands alone (#8 Snack)

One of my cardinal low-fat eating rules has just been broken—never eat cheese alone. According to the survey results, the eighth most popular snack is eating cheese alone. Make your cheese snack healthier by selecting from the great tasting reduced-fat cheeses with 3 to 5 grams of fat per ounce (reduced-fat Laughing Cow, reduced-fat sharp cheddar or Monterey Jack, part-skim Jarlsberg, reduced-fat Swiss, etc.) Second, enjoy your reduced-fat cheese with something low in fat like bread, fat-free or low-fat crackers, potatoes, or other vegetables.

Peanut butter (#20 Snack)

What goes for cheese goes double for peanut butter. At 16 grams of fat per 2-tablespoon serving, you can't afford to eat peanut butter alone, or worse yet, on a high-fat cracker. Instead, add your peanut butter to something low in fat like bread, fat-free or low-fat crackers, or fruit or vegetables, and spread it thin. There are several reduced-fat peanut butters on the market. I prefer Jif's version. But, it still has 12 grams of fat per 2-tablespoon serving, so spreading it thin is still important.

Crackers and chips (#5, #6, #7, and #13 Snack)

Entire supermarket aisles are devoted to these popular snack foods. Crackers and chips contain "hidden fat" because you can't easily see the fat in them (though you can feel the fat in most chips on your oily fingers). A few years ago, pickings were pretty slim in the lower-fat cracker category. But almost overnight, the lower-fat cracker cruncher suddenly has a shopping cart full of choices.

The cracker "dinosaurs"—Ritz, Wheat Thins, Cheez Its, Triscuits, etc.—have hopped on the lower-fat bandwagon. You know you're making progress when the most popular crackers come out with a reduced-fat cracker. And best of all, you barely notice a difference in taste.

Crackers (each brand contains 5 grams of fat or less per serving)

	Fat (gm)	Calories	Sodium (mg)
Cheez-It Reduced Fat 40% less fat, 30 crackers	4.5	130	280
Cheese Nips, Reduced Fat, 31 crackers	3.5	130	310
Garden Crisps-Vegetable 40% less fat, 15 crackers	3.5	130	290
Harvest Crisps Italian Herb, 13 crackers	3.5	130	460
Hi Ho Reduced Fat 40% less fat, 10 crackers	5	140	280
Krispy Fat Free, 5 crackers	60	0	135
Munch 'ems 33% Reduced Fat, 33 crackers	3.5	130	390
Pepperidge Farm Cracked Pepper Water Crackers, 10 crackers	2	120	180
Premium Fat Free Saltines, 5 crackers	0	50	130
Premium Low Sodium Saltines, 5 crackers	1	60	35
Premium Unsalted Tops, 5 crackers	1.5	60	135
Ritz Reduced Fat 35% less fat, 5 crackers	2.5	70	135

39

Crackers Continued

	Fat (gm)	Calories	Sodium (mg)
SnackWell's Classic Garden 75% less fat, 6 crackers	1	60	140
SnackWell's Cracked Pepper, 7 crackers	0	60	150
SnackWell's Cheese Crackers 74% less fat, 38 crackers	2	130	340
SnackWell's Wheat Crackers, 10 crackers	0	120	340
SnackWell's French Onion, 32 crackers	2	120	290
SnackWell's Zesty Cheese, 32 crackers	2	120	350
Stoned Wheat Thins (by Red Oval Farms), 4 crackers	3	120	140
Stoned Wheat Thins Sesame & Onion, 4 crackers	5	140	270
Townhouse Reduced Fat (by Keebler), 12 crackers	4	140	360
Triscuit Reduced Fat 40% less fat, 8 wafers	3	130	180
Wheat Thins Reduced Fat 30% less fat, 18 crackers	4	120	220
Wheatables Reduced Fat 50% less fat, 29 crackers	3.5	130	320
Wheatables Reduced Fat Ranch, 27 crackers	4.5	130	370

Note: Ry Krisp, Wasa, and Melba Toast crackers have always been, and still are, low in fat.

40

Chips (each brand contains 7 grams of fat or less per serving)

	Fat (gm)	Calories	Sodium (mg)
Bugles Crisp Baked 67% less fat (1 oz or 1 1/2 cups)	2.5	130	380
Eagle Restaurant Style Tortilla Rounds or Strips 100% white corn (1 oz)	6	140	70-80
Keebler Fat Free Knots 33% less sodium (1 oz)	0	110	350
Lays Reduced-Fat Potato Chips (1 oz)	6.7	140	160
Lays Low-Fat Potato Crisps (1 oz)	1.5	110	220
Mr. Phipps Tater Crisps BBQ, 23 crisps (1 oz)	4	130	270
Mr. Phipps Tater Crisps Original, 21 crisps (1 oz)	4.5	120	220
Mr. Phipps Tater Crisps Sour Cream 'n Onion (1 oz)	4	130	210
Mr. Phipps Pretzel Chips Fat Free, 16 chips (1 oz)	0	100	630
Mr. Phipps Pretzel Chips Lower Sodium (1 oz)	2.5	120	410
Mr. Phipps Pretzel Chips Original, 16 chips (1 oz)	2.5	120	630
Mister Salty Fat Free Pretzels 30% less sodium (1 oz)	0	110	400
Munch 'ems Southwestern Style Cracker Chips (1 oz)	4	140	260
Rold Gold Fat Free Pretzels 33% less sodium (1 oz)	0	110	340

Chips Continued	Fat (gm)	Calories	Sodium (mg)
Ruffles Reduced Fat Potato Chips (1 oz)	6.7	140	130
Sun Chips Original (1 oz)	6	140	115
Tostitos 100% White Corn Restaurant Style Tortilla Chips (1 oz)	6	130	80
Tostitos Baked Reduced Fat Cool Ranch Tortilla Chips(1 oz)	3	120	170
Tostitos Baked Low Fat Tortilla Chips (1 oz)	1	110	140

Cereal (#10 Snack)

Cereal can be a great snack selection if you pick a low-sugar, low-fat, high-fiber cereal. And today, there are more of these healthful types of cereal than ever before.

The granola types of cereal are often high in fat. For the rest of the cereal aisle, it's the sugar content that separates the good from the not-so-good cereals. It's not that the really high-sugar cereals are bad, they're just more like candy than cereal. The following table lists low-fat cereals that make great snacks right from the box. Plus, they have 40 percent or less calories from sugar. Not all cereals that qualify are included in this list—just ones I think are suitable snacks. Grams of fiber are also included for your information.

Cereal	Calories	Fat (gm)	Sugar (gm)	% Calories from sugar	Fiber (gm)
Apple Cinnamon Cheerios, 3/4 cup	120	2.5	12	40%	1
Cheerios, 1 cup	110	2	1	4%	1
Crispix, 1 cup	110	0	4	15%	1
Crunchy Corn Bran, 3/4 cup	90	1	6	27%	5
Frosted Mini-Wheats Bite-size, 1 cup	190	1	12	25	6
Golden Grahams, 3/4 cup	120	1	11	37%	1
Honey Comb, 1 1/3 cup	110	0	11	40%	1
Honey Graham Oh's, 3/4 cup	110	2	11	40%	1
Honey Nut Cheerios, 1 cup	120	1.5	11	37%	2
Kellogg's Low-fat Granola w/raisins, 2/3 cup	210	3	16	30%	3
Kellogg's Low-fat Granola w/o raisins, 1/2 cup	210	3	16	30%	3
Kix, 1 1/3 cups	120	0.5	3	10%	1
Muesli (Ralston) Low-fat Raspberry with Almonds, 3/4 cup	220	3	14	25%	4
Muesli Cranberry with Walnuts, 3/4 cup	220	3	14	25%	4
Muesli Sweet Raisin & Date, 3/4 cup	220	3	14	25%	4

43

Cereal Continued	Calories	Fat (gm)	Sugar (gm)	% Calories from sugar	Fiber (gm)
Quaker Oat Life-Cinnamon, 1 cup	190	2	14	29%	4
Quaker Oat Squares, 1 cup	220	2.5	9	16%	4
Rice Krispies, 1 1/4 cups	110	0	3	11%	1
Shredded Wheat, Spoon-size, 1 cup	170	0.5	0	0	5
Sun Crunchers, 1 cup	210	3	16	30%	3
Triples, 1 cup	120	1	6	20%	<1

Granola bars in the 21st century (#20 Snack)

Here's a Double Jeopardy answer for you. "A 1970s snack sensation that has transformed itself for a new century." The question is: What are granola bars? Where there once were a couple of granola bar choices on the supermarket shelf, there now are more than 20. You can choose between chewy, crunchy, or chocolate covered. You can opt for granola bars that are low or high in fat. And flavors range from the more traditional apple cinnamon to raspberry with almonds, chocolate chip, or peanut butter.

Granola bars with no more than 4 grams of fat and 40 percent calories from sugar per bar are listed below. I've also included a few breakfast and snack bars that meet the same criteria. Be sure and check out the weight of each bar; in some brands, one bar is equal to no more than four bites, in which case you'll probably eat two bars.

Granola Bars (per bar)	Calories	Fat (gm)	Sugar (gm)	% Calories from sugar	Fiber (gm)
Kellogg's Low-Fat Crunchy Almond & Brown Sugar, 21 gm	80	1.5	7	35%	1
Kudos Blueberry or Strawberry, 20 gm	80	1.5	7	35%	1
Mighty Morphin, 28 gm	130	4	10	31%	2
Nature Valley Low-Fat Chewy (Oatmeal Raisin, Apple Brown Sugar, Honey Nut, Triple Berry), 28 gm	110	2	7	25%	1
Nature Valley Low-Fat Chewy Chocolate Chip, 28 gm	110	2	6	22%	1
Nature Valley Crunchy Oats 'n Honey or Cinnamon, 23.5 gm	105	4	6	23%	1
Quaker Chewy Low-Fat Chocolate Chunk, 28 gm	110	2	9	33%	1
Quaker Chewy Low-Fat Apple Berry, 28 gm	110	2	10	36%	1

45

Breakfast and Snack Bars	Calories	Fat (gm)	Sugar (gm)	% Calories from sugar	Fiber (gm)
Kellogg's Low-Fat Pop-Tarts (Cherry, Blueberry, Strawberry), 52 gm	190	3	19	40%	na
NutriGrain (Raspberry, Blueberry, Apple Cinnamon, Peach, Strawberry), 37 gm	140	3	12	34%	1

Note: SnackWell's fat-free cereal bars didn't make the list because they contain 57% calories from sugar.

Ice cream—not just for summer (#3 Snack)

The survey results prove something I've always known. Ice cream is one of our favorite desserts and snacks, no matter what the season.

Recently, the kids and I have been experimenting with our new ice cream maker, inventing luscious low-fat frozen yogurts and ice creams in the comfort of our own kitchen. Every family member came up with a new flavor of ice cream, frozen yogurt, or sorbet they wanted to try. (The results of this homemade ice cream experiment can be found in the snack recipes section of this cookbook!)

Even if you don't have the interest or equipment to make homemade low-fat ice cream, the supermarket shelf offers you more ice cream choices than ever before. I was pleased when I discovered that most ice creams and frozen bars and treats now list the grams of sugar on their label. Before, I just made sure sugar wasn't the first item on the ingredient list. After all, ice cream should be a milk product. Call me a purist, but more milk than sugar should be added to ice cream. Fat-free and low-fat ice creams with sugar listed as the first ingredient, are so sweet they make my teeth hurt.

In the interest of preserving the dairy side of the ice cream ingredient equation (and achy teeth), only those low-fat ice creams with no more than 50 percent calories from sugar are listed in the following table. I know 50 percent still sounds high, but even at this cutoff we were leaving out lots of ice cream brands and flavors. The following ice creams also contain no more than 5 grams of fat per half cup serving.

Ice Cream	Calories	Fat (gm)	Sugar (gm)	% Calories from sugar
Breyer's Premium Light or Reduced Fat: Natural Vanilla, 1/2 cup	130	4.5	15	46%
Praline Almond Crunch, 1/2 cup	140	5	17	49%
Dannon Pure Indulgence: Coco-Nut Fudge, 1/2 cup	160	3	16	40%
Vanilla Raspberry Truffles, 1/2 cup	150	3	18	48%
Dannon Fat-Free Light: Cherry Vanilla, 1/2 cup	90	0	8	36%
Cappuccino, 1/2 cup	80	0	6	30%
Dreyer's (or Edy's) Low-Fat Ice Cream: Cookies 'n Cream, 1/2 cup	110	2	13	47%
Dreyer's (or Edy's) Grand Light: Vanilla, 1/2 cup	100	4	11	44%

47

Ice Cream Continued	Calories	Fat (gm)	Sugar (gm)	% Calories from sugar
Dreyer's (or Edy's) Rocky Road, 1/2 cup	120	5	12	40%
Dreyer's (or Edy's) Frozen Yogurt: Cookies & Cream, 1/2 cup	120	4	15	50%
Haagen Dazs Frozen Yogurt: Coffee, 1/2 cup	150	2.5	18	48%
Healthy Choice Ice Cream: Cappuccino Chocolate Chunk, 1/2 cup	120	2	14	47%

Do you know a cookie monster? (#4 Snack)

Whether you grew up counting the chips in your chocolate chip cookie, twisting off and licking your Oreo, or making cookies with your mom or grandmother, the mere thought of cookies no doubt conjures up feelings of comfort. So it's no surprise cookies are the fourth most popular snack food in America. They're familiar, can be eaten with your hands, and, thanks to commercial cookie companies, require no more talent than opening a bag or box.

For years we chose our cookies from the supermarket wearing nutritional blinders. It was only recently that cookie companies started including calorie and fat information on the packages. Were you as shocked as I was to find that our favorite cookies—the ones we had enjoyed for years—contained whopping amounts of fat? Who would have guessed that two Mystic Mint cookies contain eight grams of fat. The good news is there are many cookies in the supermarket that aren't too bad in the fat department.

When I conducted my research in the cookie aisle of my supermarket, I was looking for lower-fat cookies that did not list sugar as the first ingredient. After all, these are supposed to be "cookies" with flour as the major ingredient, not "confections" made from mostly sugar. But the cookie label has taken one more giant step forward—cookies now list grams of sugar per serving, which is a more accurate way to evaluate sugar content than looking at the ingredient list.

No one can eat just one cookie (a good tasting one, anyway). So, the nutrients listed in the following table are for about 2 ounces or at least two cookies. The cookies contain no more than 3.5 grams of fat per ounce (or 7 grams of fat per 2-ounce serving) and no more than 40% calories from sugar.

Cookies	Calories	Fat (gm)	Sugar (gm)	% Calories from sugar
Bakery Wagon Cookies:				
Iced Molasses, 2 cookies (48 gm)	180	4	18	40%
Apple Filled Oatmeal, 2 (48 gm)	180	4	16	36%
Soft Iced Oatmeal, 2 (48 gm)	200	4	18	36%
Soft Oatmeal, 2 (48 gm)	200	5	18	36%
Raspberry Filled Oatmeal, 2 (48 gm)	180	4	16	36%

Cookies Continued	Calories	Fat (gm)	Sugar (gm)	% Calories from sugar
Elfin Delights Reduced Fat Chocolate with Vanilla Creme Cookies, 5 (57 gm)	250	5.8	20	32%
Keebler Reduced Fat Vanilla Wafers, 16 (62 gm)	260	7	22	34%
Mother's Fig Bars, 3 (66 gm)	240	6	21	35%
Nabisco Ginger Snaps, 8 (56 gm)	240	5	20	33%
SnackWell's Reduced Fat Cookies:				
Mini Chocolate Chip, 26 (58 gm)	260	7	20	31%
Creme Sandwich, 4 (52 gm)	220	5	20	36%
Sunshine Golden Fruit Cookies:				
Cranberry Biscuits, 3 (60 gm)	210	3	21	40%
Apple Biscuits, 3 (60 gm)	210	3	21	40%
Raisin Biscuits, 3 (60 gm)	240	4.5	21	35%
Sunshine Reduced Fat Vienna Fingers:				
Chocolate, 4 (58 gm)	240	7	22	37%
Regular, 4 (58 gm)	260	7	20	31%

Light Snacks

Orange Julliette

2 cups orange juice
1/2 cup fat-free egg substitute
3/4 tsp vanilla extract
3 Tbsp granulated sugar
1 heaping cup ice

Combine all ingredients in a blender set on high speed for
exactly 1 minute. Makes 2 drinks.

Nutritional analysis per serving:

Calories 217, Cholesterol 0, Sodium 112 mg

% calories from:

Protein 16%, Carbohydrate 82%, Fat 2% (0.5 gm fat)

Fruity Fruit Dip

1/2 cup fat-free cream cheese

1/2 cup marshmallow cream

1/8 cup strawberry jam (or other berry jam)

Mix ingredients in small food processor or with mixer until smooth. Serve with assorted fruit slices (apples, peaches, bananas, etc.) Makes 5, 1/8-cup servings.

Nutritional analysis per 1/8-cup serving:

Calories 133, Cholesterol 2 mg, Sodium 160 mg

% calories from:

Protein 13%, Carbohydrate 87%, Fat 0

Peanut Butter Vegetable Spread

1/4 cup reduced-fat peanut butter (e.g., reduced-fat Jif)

1/4 cup fat-free cream cheese

2 Tbsp marshmallow creme

Blend all ingredients together until smooth using small food processor or mixer. Spread on celery, cucumber, or carrot sticks (or any other vegetable you like). Makes 3 servings of spread.

Nutritional analysis per serving of spread only:

Calories 163, Fiber 1.3 gm, Cholesterol 2 mg, Sodium 290 mg

% calories from:

Protein 20%, Carbohydrate 36%, Fat 44% (8 gm fat)

Quick Ranch Dip (for vegetables)

1 packet (1.6 oz) Ranch Dressing powder
1/4 cup light or nonfat sour cream
1 1/2 cups 1% or 2% low-fat milk
1/4 cup reduced-fat or nonfat mayonnaise
Assorted raw vegetables for dipping

Combine all dip ingredients in a small bowl. Beat with wire whisk or mixer until smooth and creamy. The dressing will thicken in refrigerator and will stay fresh about 3 weeks when kept covered in the refrigerator. Makes 2 cups.

Nutritional analysis per 1/4 cup of dip (approximate values):
Calories 40, Cholesterol 6.5 mg, Sodium 376 mg

% calories from:
Protein 22%, Carbohydrate 42%, Fat 36% (1.6 gm fat)

Peanut Butter Krispy Treats

4 cups miniature marshmallows

1/4 cup creamy peanut butter (reduced-fat creamy peanut butter can also be used)

2 Tbsp corn syrup

6 cups Kellogg's Rice Krispies cereal

No-stick cooking spray

Spray a 4-cup glass measuring cup or medium sized glass bowl with no-stick cooking spray. Add marshmallows, peanut butter, and corn syrup to cup or bowl. Microwave on high for 2 minutes. Stir until smooth. Microwave additional minute if needed. Spray the inside of a large bowl with no-stick cooking spray. Add cereal. Drizzle peanut butter-marshmallow mixture evenly over the top. Stir to combine. Coat a 9 x 9 x 2" or 9 x 13 x 2" pan with no-stick cooking spray. Press mixture evenly into pan using a spatula or waxed paper that has been coated with no-stick cooking spray. Refrigerate. Cut into 25 large squares.

Nutritional analysis per square:

Calories 73, Cholesterol 0, Sodium 101 mg

% calories from:

Protein 7%, Carbohydrate 78%, Fat 15% (1.2 gm fat)

Peanut Butter Banana

1 banana

2 Tbsp reduced-fat peanut butter (I prefer Jif)

Something to roll banana in, such as cake decorating sprinkles, Rice Krispies, etc.

Peel banana. Set on piece of foil and place in freezer for 1 hour. Meanwhile remove peanut butter from refrigerator and bring to room temperature (so it's more spreadable). Use 2 tablespoons of the peanut butter and a dinner knife to spread peanut butter all around the banana. Roll in food item of choice (sprinkles, Rice Krispies, etc.). Place on wooden stick or Popsicle stick if desired and place in refrigerator for 1 hour. It's ready to eat! Serves 2.

Nutritional analysis per serving:

Calories 147, Fiber 2 gm, Cholesterol 0, Sodium 125 mg

% calories from:

Protein 10%, Carbohydrate 55%, Fat 35% (6 gm fat)

Strawberry-Yogurt Mousse

1 strawberry or raspberry Jell-o gelatin snack cup, or 1/3 cup prepared Jell-o

1 cup crushed fresh or slice frozen strawberries, unsweetened

1 6-oz container low-fat strawberry yogurt

1/2 cup light Cool Whip

Break Jell-o up into pieces with a fork. Add Jell-o, strawberries, yogurt, and Cool Whip to mixing bowl, and beat on low until evenly blended. Spoon into serving cups. Refrigerate until needed. Makes at least 3 servings.

Nutritional analysis per serving (if 3 per recipe):

Calories 115, Fiber 1.5 gm, Cholesterol 2 mg, Sodium 47 mg

% calories from:

Protein 11%, Carbohydrate 73%, Fat 16% (2 gm fat)

Yogurt Granola Parfait

1 6-oz container 1% low-fat fruit flavored yogurt, such as
lemon, strawberry-banana

1/2 cup Lite Cool Whip, thawed in refrigerator

1/2 cup Kellogg's low-fat granola (or similar)

In small bowl, blend yogurt and Cool Whip together with
a spoon until smooth. Spoon 1/4 of mixture into bottom of
one parfait glass (or similar) and repeat with second glass.
Sprinkle 1/8 cup of granola over yogurt mixture in each
glass. Spoon half of remaining yogurt mixture on top of
granola in each glass. Top with 1/8 cup of granola for each
of the glasses. Serve immediately. If storing in refrigerator, cover tightly with plastic wrap. Makes 2 parfaits.

Nutritional analysis per parfait:

Calories 208, Cholesterol 5 mg, Sodium 103 mg

% calories from:

Protein 13%, Carbohydrate 71%, Fat 16% (3.7 gm fat)

Caramel Corn

6 quarts plain popped popcorn (no added fat)

3 Tbsp butter

1/2 cup molasses

6 Tbsp apple juice

2 Tbsp vanilla extract

1/2 cup light corn syrup

2 cups brown sugar

1 tsp salt

1 tsp baking soda

1 cup Planters reduced-fat honey roasted peanuts (optional)

No-stick cooking spray

Place popped popcorn in the largest bowl you can find; set aside. Line two large baking sheets with foil. Spray foil generously with no-stick cooking spray. Preheat oven to 200°.

In a large non-stick saucepan, melt butter over medium heat. Add molasses, apple juice, vanilla extract, corn syrup, brown sugar, and salt. Heat to boiling, and let boil 5 minutes, stirring frequently.

Remove from heat, and stir in baking soda (the mixture will foam and double in size). Pour half of mixture over popcorn, and toss gently. Repeat with remaining mixture.

Stir in peanuts if desired. Spread onto the prepared baking sheet.

Bake for 1 hour, stirring every 20 minutes. Remove from oven and let cool on pans. Store in tins or airtight containers. Makes 10, 2-cup servings.

Nutritional analysis per 2-cup serving:

Calories 307, Fiber 3 gm, Cholesterol 9 mg, Sodium 265 mg

% calories from:

Protein 3%, Carbohydrate 84%, Fat 13% (4.4 gm fat)

Parmesan Popcorn

Although the butter spray listed below contains water, because you are spraying it (dispersing the water droplets over a greater surface area) and not pouring it (as is the case when diet margarine is melted and used), the popcorn doesn't become too soggy.

    4 cups plain popcorn (no added fat)
    I Can't Believe It's Not Butter spray, approximately
        10 sprays
    1/8 cup finely grated Parmesan cheese

Spread popcorn out in shallow pan (a 9 x 9" baking pan will do fine). Spray generously with I Can't Believe It's Not Butter spray. Sprinkle Parmesan cheese over the top. Pour into serving bowl. Makes 1 snack serving.

Nutritional analysis per serving:

Calories 178, Fiber 5 gm, Cholesterol 9 mg, Sodium 224 mg

% calories from:

Protein 20%, Carbohydrate 55%, Fat 25% (5 gm fat)

Microwave Cheese Fondue

Great for dipping vegetables, apples, and fresh French or sour-dough bread.

> 2 Tbsp Gold Medal Wondra flour
> 1/4 tsp salt
> 1/8 tsp pepper
> 3/4 cup low-fat milk, divided
> 1 clove garlic (optional)
> 2 Tbsp white wine (optional)
> 1/2 cup firmly packed grated reduced-fat sharp cheddar cheese (at least 2 oz)
> 1/3 to 1/2 of a sourdough or French bread loaf (about 8 oz)

Mix flour, salt, and pepper in medium microwavable bowl. Add 1/4 cup of milk, and stir. Add remaining milk, garlic, and wine (if desired), and stir until smooth. Microwave uncovered on high for 2 minutes; stir. Microwave 2 to 3 minutes, stirring every minute until nicely thickened. Add cheese, and stir until melted and smooth. Makes almost a cup of fondue sauce (about 3 servings).

63

Nutritional analysis per serving (including bread):
Calories 334, Fiber 1.5 gm, Cholesterol 21 mg, Sodium 746 mg

% calories from:
Protein 18%, Carbohydrate 61%, Fat 21% (7.5 gm fat)

Cheese Bread

2 oz reduced-fat sharp cheddar cheese, grated

3 Tbsp shredded Parmesan cheese

1 clove garlic, crushed or minced

3 Tbsp low-fat, reduced-fat, or fat-free mayonnaise

1/2 tsp oregano flakes (dried)

6 slices sourdough bread (sliced French, Italian, or other bread will also work)

Paprika to taste

Mix first five ingredients together in small bowl until evenly blended. Spread on bread. Sprinkle with paprika to taste. Broil bread, watching carefully, until cheese bubbles. Makes 6 slices.

Nutritional analysis per slice:

Calories 152, Fiber 0.6 gm, Cholesterol 12 mg, Sodium 320 mg

64

% calories from:

Protein 19%, Carbohydrate 54%, Fat 27% (4.5 gm fat)

Mandarin Orange Sorbet

2 15-oz cans mandarin oranges, drained

3/4 cup orange juice

1/2 cup water

2/3 cup sugar

2 egg whites

In a saucepan over medium heat, combine mandarin oranges, orange juice, water, and sugar. Stir until sugar is dissolved. Puree briefly in food processor or blender, then chill thoroughly in refrigerator. Beat egg whites until soft peaks form. Whisk egg whites into mandarin orange mixture. Continue as per instructions for your ice cream maker. Makes about 6 servings.

NOTE: This sorbet tastes great with mini chocolate chips stirred in when sorbet is ready or with chocolate syrup drizzled on top of each serving.

Nutritional analysis per serving:

Calories 144, Fiber 2 gm, Cholesterol 0, Sodium 24 mg

% calories from:

Protein 5%, Carbohydrate 94%, Fat 1% (0.1 gm fat)

65

Chocolate and Peanut Butter Ice Milk

Make one day before:

3 1/2 cups whole milk, divided

2 egg yolks

1 cup sugar

1/3 cup cocoa

1 1/2 tsp vanilla

12 tsp reduced-fat Jif peanut butter (or similar); add less
peanut butter if you want a weaker peanut butter flavor

Beat 1 1/2 cups of milk and egg yolks together. Blend in
sugar. Cook over medium-low heat, stirring constantly,
until thick enough to coat the spoon. Remove from heat
and gently sift cocoa into the mixture. Beat well until
blended. Cool. Stir in remaining milk and vanilla. Mix
well, and refrigerate overnight. Continue to make chocolate ice milk as per the instructions for your ice cream
maker. When the chocolate ice cream is almost ready,
drop in peanut butter, teaspoon by teaspoon. If your ice
cream maker doesn't automatically mix and blend in the
peanut butter, stir in by hand until well mixed. Makes 8
servings.

Nutritional analysis per serving:

Calories 233, Fiber 1.5 gm, Cholesterol 68 mg, Sodium 142 mg

% calories from:

Protein 14% Carbohydrate 63%, Fat 33% (8.5 gm fat)

Lemon Drop Frozen Yogurt

About 30 lemon drops

2 cups low-fat lemon yogurt

1/2 cup lemon juice

3/4 cup whole milk (low-fat can also be used)

1/2 cup light corn syrup

Crush lemon drops into coarse crumbs in food processor or blender. Set aside. In mixing bowl, combine remaining ingredients. Mix well. Continue to make frozen yogurt as per the instructions for your ice cream maker. When frozen yogurt is just about ready to serve, add crushed lemon drops. If your ice cream maker doesn't automatically blend them in, stir them in by hand. Makes 8 servings.

Nutritional analysis per serving:

Calories 193, Fiber 0.1 gm, Cholesterol 5 mg, Sodium 63 mg

% calories from:

Protein 7%, Carbohydrate 86%, Fat 7% (1.5 gm fat)

67

Oreo-Espresso Ice Cream

1 1/2 cups 2% low-fat milk

2 to 3 Tbsp instant espresso powder

1 14-oz can low-fat sweetened condensed milk

1/3 cup chocolate syrup

9 to 12 reduced-fat Oreo cookies, crumbled lightly in food processor or by hand

Prepare ice cream maker as directed in your instructions. In mixing bowl, beat low-fat milk and instant espresso to combine. Add sweetened condensed milk and chocolate syrup, and beat until combined. Pour into ice cream maker and continue as directed in your ice cream maker instructions. Once ice cream is ready (frozen and fluffy), add in, or stir in by hand, the cookie pieces. Makes 8 servings.

Nutritional analysis per serving:

Calories 260, Fiber 0.4 gm, Cholesterol 10.5 mg, Sodium 165 mg

% calories from:

Protein 10%, Carbohydrate 73%, Fat 17% (5 gm fat)

Chocolate-Covered Cherry Frozen Yogurt

3 6-oz cartons low-fat cherry yogurt

1/4 cup cherry or berry syrup (or use orange juice)

1/4 cup orange juice

3/4 cup low-fat milk

1/2 cup light corn syrup

6 chocolate covered cherries, frozen then quartered, or 5 special dark miniature chocolate bars (or similar), chopped

In a mixing bowl, combine all ingredients except chocolate covered cherries, and mix well. Pour into ice cream maker and continue as directed in your ice cream maker instructions. Once ice cream is ready (frozen and fluffy), add in, or stir in by hand, the chocolate covered cherries (or chocolate pieces). Makes 6 servings.

Nutritional analysis per serving:

Calories 257, Fiber 0.4 gm, Cholesterol 6 mg, Sodium 85 mg

% calories from:

Protein 8%, Carbohydrate 79%, Fat 13% (4 gm fat)

69

Old Fashioned Chocolate Malt

I just had to include a light version of a chocolate malt since this is one of my favorite treats (and my husband's).

1 heaping Tbsp Carnation malted milk powder
1 Tbsp cocoa
2 Tbsp chocolate syrup
6 Tbsp skim milk (or 1% or 2% low-fat milk)
1 cup low-fat vanilla ice cream
1/2 cup crushed ice

In a small bowl or cup, mix malted milk powder with cocoa. Add to blender or food processor. Add remaining ingredients. Blend until smooth. Serve immediately. Makes 1 large or 2 small shakes.

Nutritional analysis per small shake:
Calories 195, Cholesterol 35 mg, Sodium 166 mg

% calories from:
Protein 12%, Carbohydrate 66%, Fat 22% (5.2 gm fat)

Trail Mix

1 cup low-fat Muesli cereal

1/3 cup Planters reduced-fat honey roasted peanuts

1/2 cup raisins

Place ingredients in a medium sized bowl or storage size zip-lock bag, and toss to blend. Makes 2 servings.

Nutritional analysis per serving (using Ralston Blueberry Muesli with pecans):

Calories 295, Fiber 5 gm, Cholesterol 0, Sodium 170 mg

% calories from:

Protein 9%, Carbohydrate 77%, Fat 14% (4.7 gm fat)

Loop De Loop Snack

1 cup Multi Grain Cheerios
3/4 cup Honey Graham Oh's
1/2 cup Fruit Loops (or similar)

Place ingredients in a medium sized bowl or storage sized zip-lock bag, and toss to blend. Makes 1 serving.

Nutritional analysis per serving:

Calories 280, Fiber 5 gm, Cholesterol 0, Sodium 550 mg

% calories from:

Protein 9%, Carbohydrate 78%, Fat 13% (4 gm fat)

Low-Fat Crispix Mix

7 cups Crispix cereal

1/2 cup Planters reduced-fat peanuts

1 1/2 to 2 cups pretzels

1 1/2 Tbsp butter or margarine, melted

1 1/2 Tbsp maple syrup

1/4 tsp garlic powder

1/4 tsp onion powder

2 tsp lemon juice

4 tsp Worcestershire sauce

Preheat oven to 250°. Combine cereal, peanuts, and pretzels in 13 x 9 x 2" baking pan. Set aside. Stir together butter, maple syrup, garlic powder, onion powder, lemon juice, and Worcestershire sauce. Gently stir mixture over cereal mixture until coated.

Bake for about 45 minutes, stirring every 15 minutes. Spread on paper towels to cool. Store in airtight container. Makes 9 cups.

Microwave directions: In a large microwave-safe bowl, combine cereal, peanuts, and pretzels. Follow directions above. Microwave at high 4 minutes, stirring after 2 minutes. Spread on paper towels to cool. Store in airtight container.

Nutritional analysis per cup:

Calories 164, Fiber 2 gm, Cholesterol 5 mg, Sodium 372 mg

% calories from:

Protein 7%, Carbohydrate 73%, Fat 18% (3.4 gm fat)

73

Granola Snack Bars

1/4 cup butter or margarine, softened

1/4 cup fat-free cream cheese

2 Tbsp molasses

1 cup brown sugar

1 egg

1/4 cup fat-free egg substitute

1 Tbsp vanilla

1 cup flour (white or wheat)

1 Tbsp baking powder

1 tsp salt

2 1/2 cups Kellogg's low-fat granola (or similar)

No-stick cooking spray

Preheat oven to 350°. Coat a 9 x 9" baking pan with no-stick cooking spray. In mixer bowl, beat butter and cream cheese together. Add molasses and brown sugar. Beat in egg, egg substitute, and vanilla.

In separate bowl, mix flour, baking powder, salt, and granola together. Blend this flour mixture with the butter mixture. Spread batter in prepared pan, and bake for about 25 minutes or until the center is just set. Cool and cut into squares. Makes 16 squares.

Nutritional analysis per serving:

Calories 167, Fiber 1 gm (using whole wheat flour will increase the fiber to 1.6 gm), Cholesterol 21 mg, Sodium 270 mg

% calories from:

Protein 6%, Carbohydrate 73%, Fat 21% (4 gm fat)

74

Cracker Bag Snack

1 oz reduced-fat Cheese Nips (or reduced-fat Cheez It crackers)

1 oz reduced-fat Wheat Thins (or reduced-fat Wheatables)

1 oz Snackwell's French onion crackers

Put all the crackers in a storage size zip-lock bag. Shake bag to mix the crackers. If desired, fill three sandwich size bags with equal portions of the cracker medley. Makes 3, 1-ounce servings.

Nutritional analysis per serving:

Calories 123, Fiber < 1 gm, Cholesterol 0, Sodium 273 mg

% calories from:

Protein 8%, Carbohydrate 70%, Fat 22% (3.2 gm fat)

Oil-Free Bagel Chips

1 bagel, cut into about 4 thin slices
1/2 tsp garlic powder
Pinch of pepper
1 Tbsp Parmesan cheese, shredded as finely as possible
Olive oil no-stick cooking spray

Preheat oven to 325°. Place the bagel slices in a single layer on a cookie sheet. Spray the top of each piece with no-stick cooking spray. In small cup, blend garlic powder with pepper and Parmesan. Sprinkle over the bread. Bake for 5 to 10 minutes or until bagel slices are golden brown and crisp all the way through. Let the bagel chips cool. Break into smaller pieces if desired. Makes 1 serving.

Nutritional analysis per serving:

Calories 208, Fiber 1.2 gm, Cholesterol 5 mg, Sodium 416 mg

% calories from:

Protein 19%, Carbohydrate 69%, Fat 13% (2.8 gm fat)

Iced Cafe Mocha

4 ice cubes

2 level tsp instant espresso powder (available in a small
bottle in the coffee section of most supermarkets)

1 cup 1% low-fat milk, divided (nonfat or 2% may be substituted)

2 Tbsp chocolate syrup

Place ice cubes in a blender or food processor and pulse
until crushed. In small cup blend espresso powder with 2
tablespoons of the milk. Add to blender along with
remaining milk and chocolate syrup. Pulse until nicely
blended. Makes 1 drink.

Nutritional analysis per serving:

Calories 186, Fiber 1 gm, Cholesterol 10 mg, Sodium 164 mg

% calories from:

Protein 19%, Carbohydrate 69%, Fat 12% (2.7 gm fat)

Christmas Quesadilla

My daughters named this Christmas Quesadilla because of the red and green colored vegetables that go on the tortilla.

1 flour tortilla

1 oz reduced-fat Monterey Jack cheese, grated

1/2 ripe tomato, cut into chunks (1/4 cup mild or medium salsa can be substituted)

1/4 cup chopped green bell pepper

1 Tbsp roasted mild green peppers (canned Ortega peppers) (optional)

1 green onion, chopped

No-stick cooking spray (optional)

Place tortilla on microwave-safe plate. Sprinkle cheese evenly over the tortilla. Place tomato pieces, peppers, and green onion evenly over half of the tortilla. Fold the tortilla half without the vegetables over. Microwave on high for 2 minutes or until cheese bubbles.

For a crispier tortilla, coat a non-stick frying pan with no-stick cooking spray. Add prepared quesadilla, and cook over medium heat until bottom side is nicely browned. Flip it over and cook other side until browned. Makes 1 serving.

Nutritional analysis per serving:

Calories 206, Fiber 2.5 gm, Cholesterol 15 mg, Sodium 291 mg

% calories from:

Protein 21%, Carbohydrate 47%, Fat 33% (7.8 gm fat)

78

Pintos and Cheese

1/2 cup fat-free refried beans, divided (e.g., Rosarita no-fat refried beans)

2 Tbsp salsa, divided (or 1 tsp chili sauce, divided), or to taste

1 oz reduced-fat Monterey Jack cheese, grated

2 green onions, finely chopped

Spread half of beans in serving bowl. Top beans with half of the salsa. In small bowl, toss grated cheese with green onion. Sprinkle half of cheese and onion mixture over beans. Spread remaining beans over the top then add remaining salsa. Sprinkle remaining cheese and onion over the top. Microwave on high for 2 to 3 minutes or until cheese bubbles. Makes 1 serving.

NOTE: To make this more like a meal, serve it with 1 or 2 flour tortillas that have been cooked until crisp in frying pan. Just coat a non-stick frying pan with no-stick cooking spray. Cook the tortilla over medium-low heat, until bottom is light brown. Spray the top with no-stick cooking spray then flip over to brown the other side.

79

Nutritional analysis per serving (not including tortillas):
Calories 215, Fiber 6.7 gm, Cholesterol 15 mg, Sodium 749 mg

% calories from:
Protein 22%, Carbohydrate 55%, Fat 23% (5.5 gm fat)

Decadent
Late-Night Snacks
& Delectable
Desserts

Creamy Lemon Pie

1 9" baked lower-fat graham cracker pie crust
  (recipe follows)

2 egg yolks

2 Tbsp fat-free egg substitute

1 14-oz can Eagle Brand fat-free sweetened condensed
  skimmed milk (NOT evaporated milk)

1/2 cup lemon juice

Zest from 1 lemon (optional)

NOTE: You can use the leftover egg whites by whipping them until stiff, adding 3 tablespoons powdered sugar then blending it with 1 cup of whipped cream or light Cool Whip to make a lower-fat whipped topping. (Raw egg should probably not be consumed by young children and adults who have weak immune systems.)

Preheat oven to 325°. In medium mixer bowl, beat egg yolks and egg substitute with sweetened condensed milk, lemon juice, and lemon zest. Pour into prepared graham cracker crust; bake 25 minutes. Cool. Refrigerate until served. If desired, top with a dollop of light Cool Whip, light whipping cream, low-fat vanilla ice cream, or frozen yogurt. Makes 12 servings.

Nutritional analysis per serving:

Calories 189, Fiber 0.4 gm, Cholesterol 40 mg, Sodium 134 mg

% calories from:

Protein 10%, Carbohydrate 71%, Fat 19% (4 gm fat)

Graham Cracker Crust:

2 Tbsp butter or margarine

2 Tbsp low-fat sweetened condensed milk

1 Tbsp Kahlua, Light Baileys Irish Creme, etc.
  (or 1 Tbsp milk)

2 Tbsp sugar

1 1/4 cups finely crushed graham crackers (about 8 whole crackers)

No-stick cooking spray

Melt butter. Stir in condensed milk, Kahlua, and sugar. Add crushed graham crackers. Toss to mix well. Press mixture evenly into bottom of a 9" pie plate that has been coated with no-stick cooking spray. Chill about 1 hour or until firm (or bake in 375° oven for 4 minutes. Cool on wire rack before filling).

83

Light Chocolate Oatmeal Chippers

1 1/4 cups all-purpose flour

1/2 cup Nestle baking cocoa

1 tsp baking soda

1/2 tsp salt

1/2 cup butter or margarine, softened

1/2 cup fat-free cream cheese

1 cup packed brown sugar

1/2 cup granulated sugar

2 tsp vanilla extract

1 egg

1/4 cup fat-free egg substitute

1 cup Nestle Toll House milk chocolate morsels

1 3/4 cups quick or old-fashioned oats

1/2 cup chopped walnuts or pecans (optional)

No-stick cooking spray

84

Preheat oven to 375°. In small bowl, combine flour, cocoa, baking soda, and salt. In large mixing bowl, cream butter with cream cheese. Add sugars and vanilla, and blend until smooth. Add egg and egg substitute, beating well after each addition. Gradually beat in dry ingredients. Stir in chocolate chips, oats, and nuts if desired. Drop by rounded tablespoon, or cookie scoop, onto baking sheets coated with cooking spray. Bake for about 8 to 10 minutes, watching carefully. Let stand for 2 minutes. Remove to wire racks to cool completely. Makes 4 1/2 dozen cookies.

Nutritional analysis per serving:

Calories 78, Cholesterol 9 mg, Sodium 63 mg

% calories from:

Protein 6%, Carbohydrate 58%, Fat 36% (3 gm fat)

Light Tin Roof Sundae

I have fond memories of sitting in my neighborhood fountain shop eating tin roof sundaes with my teenage friends. I thought my tin roof days were over. Then, while I was writing this book, a nutritional miracle occurred. Fat-free hot fudge sauce and less-fat peanuts became available, and I couldn't resist making up a less-fat tin roof sundae.

> 1/8 cup Smuckers light hot fudge (if not available, substitute chocolate syrup)
>
> 3/4 cup light vanilla ice cream (with 4 gm fat per 1/2 cup)
>
> 1/8 cup Planters reduced-fat honey roasted peanuts
>
> Squirt of canned whipped cream (or similar), about 2 Tbsp worth

Spoon hot fudge into microwave-safe custard cup (or similar). Heat on defrost setting for about 1 minute. Spoon half of the hot fudge into bottom of small parfait dish (or other narrow serving dish). Top with half of the ice cream. Sprinkle half of the peanuts over the top. Top that with the remaining ice cream then the remaining hot fudge. Sprinkle the rest of the peanuts over the hot fudge, and top with a squirt of canned whipped cream. Makes 1 fabulous serving.

85

Nutritional analysis per serving:

Calories 315, Fiber 1 gm, Cholesterol 47 mg, Sodium 200 mg

% calories from:

Protein 10%, Carbohydrate 60%, Fat 30% (10.5 gm fat) — without the whipped cream the sundae contains 8.5 gm fat.

Chocolate Mint Cookies

These cookies are so good, I even thought about trying to sell the recipe to a local commercial bakery company.

1 1/2 cups flour
1 1/2 tsp baking powder
1/4 tsp salt (optional)
1 cup Nestle Toll House mint flavored semi-sweet chocolate morsels
3 Tbsp low-fat milk
3 Tbsp butter or margarine, softened
2/3 cup sugar
1 1/2 tsp vanilla extract
1 egg
2 Tbsp fat-free egg substitute (or 1 egg white)
No-stick cooking spray

86

Combine flour, baking powder, and salt; set aside. Melt chocolate chips with milk over low heat in small non-stick saucepan. In large mixer bowl, beat butter with sugar. Add chocolate mixture and vanilla, and beat to blend. Add egg and egg substitute, and beat until smooth. Add flour mixture.

Split dough into fourths and wrap each fourth in plastic wrap. Freeze until firm (about 20 minutes.) Preheat oven to 350°. Shape each portion of dough into about 9 1-inch balls, and place on a cookie sheet that has been coated with no-stick cooking spray. Bake for about 10 minutes, watching carefully. Makes about 36 cookies.

NOTE: One or all of the dough portions can be left in the freezer and made within a couple weeks. Just let each portion of dough thaw on the kitchen counter for about 15 minutes then proceed to shape into 1-inch balls.

Nutritional analysis per cookie:

Calories 71, Fiber 0.3 gm, Cholesterol 9 mg, Sodium 28 mg

% calories from:

Protein 6%, Carbohydrate 58%, Fat 37% (3 gm fat)

Apricot Rum Raisin Rice Pudding

1 cup long-grain white rice, uncooked

4 cups water

4 cups 2% low-fat milk

2/3 cup sugar

1 Tbsp butter

3 Tbsp maple syrup

1 Tbsp vanilla extract

1/3 cup raisins

4 to 5 Tbsp water

1 to 2 Tbsp rum

3 Tbsp low-sugar apricot preserves

Light whipping cream or light Cool Whip as garnish (optional)

Blanch the rice in 4 cups boiling water for 5 minutes. Drain water from rice. In a large saucepan, combine the rice with milk, sugar, butter, maple syrup, and vanilla. Over medium heat, bring the rice mixture to a boil, then reduce the heat to low. Cover and simmer until rice is tender and the mixture has thickened (about 45 minutes). Stir a few times to prevent sticking.

Pour the mixture into a bowl to cool. Refrigerate until cold, stirring occasionally. While rice is cooling, place raisins, 4 tablespoons water, and 2 tablespoons rum (or 5 tablespoons water and 1 tablespoon rum) in a small bowl. Microwave on high for about 2 minutes, stir, and microwave an additional 2 minutes, or until raisins are plump and liquid is almost completely absorbed.

Once the rice mixture is cold, stir in the raisins and apricot preserves. Chill in refrigerator until needed. For garnish, top each serving with a dollop of light whipping cream, light Cool Whip, or a splash of half-and-half if desired. Makes about 8 servings.

NOTE: You can make this pudding up to 3 days in advance; just keep it covered in the refrigerator.

Nutritional analysis per serving:

Calories 264, Fiber 1 gm, Cholesterol 9 mg, Sodium 82 mg

% calories from:

Protein 9%, Carbohydrate 81%, Fat 10% (2.8 gm fat)

Kahlua White Russian Cheesecake

If you like white Russian drinks and if you like cheesecake, you'll love this dessert!

12 oz fat-free cream cheese

12 oz light cream cheese

3/4 cup sugar

1/2 tsp salt

1 1/2 tsp vanilla extract

2 eggs

1/4 cup fat-free egg substitute

1/4 cup Kahlua

2 Tbsp vodka

2/3 cup light sour cream

2/3 cup flaked coconut, toasted (see toasting directions on package)

Caramel Nut Crust (recipe follows)

Beat cream cheese until smooth. Beat in sugar, salt and vanilla. Add eggs, one at a time, beating well after each. Add egg substitute and beat well. Stir in Kahlua and vodka. Pour into prepared crust. Set on baking sheet. Bake at 350° for 45 minutes. Cool 5 minutes. Stir sour cream then spread over cake. Sprinkle toasted coconut on top. Refrigerate. Makes about 12 servings.

Nutritional analysis per serving:

Calories 277, Fiber 0.5 gm, Cholesterol 57 mg, Sodium 506 mg

% calories from:

Protein 19%, Carbohydrate 50%, Fat 31% (9.5 gm fat)

Caramel Nut Crust:

In skillet, over low heat, stir 1 tablespoon butter and 1 tablespoon milk with 3 tablespoons sugar. Add 2 tablespoons Kahlua. Heat and stir 2 minutes. Place 28 reduced-fat vanilla wafers and 1/4 cup pecan pieces in food processor and pulse to make crumbs. Add butter mixture and pulse briefly to blend. Press in even layer in bottom of a 9" springform pan.

Pumpkin Spice Cookies

These cookies come out extra moist because of the pumpkin and extra maple syrup (to replace some of the butter). To my surprise the children who tasted these cookies loved them too — that's always a good sign.

1 cup brown sugar

4 Tbsp butter or margarine, softened

1/4 cup fat-free (or light) cream cheese

1/2 cup maple syrup

1 cup canned pumpkin

1 1/2 tsp vanilla

1 egg

2 cups flour

1 tsp baking powder

1 tsp baking soda

1 tsp ground cinnamon

1 tsp pumpkin pie spice

1/4 tsp salt

1/2 cup raisins or chocolate chips (optional)

No-stick cooking spray

Preheat oven to 350°. Beat brown sugar with butter, cream cheese, and maple syrup; set aside. In separate bowl, mix pumpkin, vanilla, and egg; set aside. In medium sized bowl, stir together flour, baking powder, baking soda, cinnamon, pumpkin pie spice, and salt. Add pumpkin mixture to butter-sugar mixture. Slowly add in flour, beating just until blended. Stir in raisins or chocolate chips if desired.

Spray cookie sheets with no-stick cooking spray. Use cookie scoop (or heaping tablespoon) to drop cookie dough onto cookie sheet. Bake for about 10 to 12 minutes (or until center of cookie springs back when touched). Makes 32 large bakery sized cookies.

Nutritional analysis per cookie:

Calories 84, Fiber 0.4 gm, Cholesterol 10 mg, Sodium 72 mg

% calories from:

Protein 5%, Carbohydrate 77%, Fat 18% (1.7 gm fat)

Quick Apple Cake

Everybody likes apple pie. But not many want to make a pie crust at the end of the day. This is an apple cake without the hassle of making a pie crust. Just mix, spread, and bake. This dessert is wonderful served warm with light vanilla ice cream or frozen yogurt.

1 egg

1/4 cup fat-free egg substitute

1 cup packed brown sugar

1 cup granulated sugar

1 Tbsp vanilla

A couple pinches salt

1 cup flour

2 tsp baking powder

5 cups peeled and thinly sliced apples

1/2 cup chopped pecans (optional)

No-stick cooking spray

94

Preheat oven to 350°. Beat egg and egg substitute in mixer bowl. Add sugars, vanilla, salt, flour, and baking powder. Mix well. Stir in apples. Add pecans if desired. Spread batter into 9 x 13" pan coated with no-stick cooking spray. Bake for about 30 to 40 minutes or until browned on top and fork inserted in center comes out clean. Serve with light vanilla ice cream or frozen yogurt if desired. Makes 10 servings.

Nutritional analysis per serving:

Calories 247, Fiber 1.5 gm, Cholesterol 21 mg, Sodium 107 mg

% calories from:

Protein 4%, Carbohydrate 93%, Fat 3% (0.8 gm fat)

Nutritional analysis per serving (including pecans):

Calories 283, Fiber 2 gm, Cholesterol 21 mg, Sodium 107 mg

% calories from:

Protein 4%, Carbohydrate 82%, Fat 14% (4.4 gm fat)

Light Cherry Wink Cookies

A Pillsbury Bake-Off favorite — made light!

1 cup sugar

6 Tbsp butter or margarine, softened (shortening can also be used)

6 Tbsp fat-free cream cheese

2 tsp vanilla

1 egg

3 Tbsp fat-free egg substitute

2 1/4 cups all purpose or unbleached flour

1 tsp baking powder

1/2 tsp baking soda

1/2 tsp salt

1/2 cup chopped pecans

1 cup raisins or chopped dates

1/3 cup chopped maraschino cherries, well drained (glace cherries can also be used)

1 1/2 cups coarsely crushed cornflakes (about 4 cups of cereal)

12 maraschino cherries, cut in half (glace cherries can also be used)

No-stick cooking spray

Preheat oven to 375°. Coat nonstick cookie sheets with no-stick cooking spray.

In large bowl, mix sugar, butter, cream cheese, vanilla, egg, and egg substitute at medium speed until well mixed. Lightly spoon flour into measuring cup; level off. In small bowl, combine flour, baking powder, baking soda, and salt; mix well. Add to sugar mixture; mix at low speed only until blended. Stir in pecans, raisins, and 1/3 cup of the chopped cherries. Place cornflakes in medium sized bowl. Use cookie scoop to scoop dough, then drop dough ball into cornflakes and roll dough around to coat. Place onto cookie sheet. Gently press cherry half into top of each cookie ball. Bake for 10 to 13 minutes or until just starting to lightly brown. Makes 24 large bakery size cookies.

Nutritional analysis per serving:

Calories 168, Fiber 1 gm, Cholesterol 17 mg, Sodium 128 mg

% calories from:

Protein 7%, Carbohydrate 68%, Fat 25% (4.7 gm fat)

Chocolate Lovers' Cheesecake
(with creamy rum topping)

Chocolate Cookie Crust:
18 reduced-fat Oreos

2 Tbsp diet margarine, melted

2 Tbsp chocolate syrup

No-stick cooking spray

Puree cookies into crumbs using a food processor. Add margarine and chocolate syrup, and pulse food processor just until blended. Press into the bottom of a springform pan that has been coated with no-stick cooking spray or into the bottom and partway up the sides of a 9" pie plate. To prevent cookie crust from sticking to your hand as you press it into the pan, sprinkle a little flour over the crust before you press, or coat your hand with no-stick cooking spray before pressing.

Creamy Rum Topping:
1/2 cup light Philadelphia cream cheese

1/2 cup fat-free Philadelphia cream cheese

1/3 cup sugar

2 tsp all-purpose flour

1 tsp rum extract

1 egg beaten with 1 Tbsp fat-free egg substitute

Beat all creamy rum topping ingredients together until smooth. Keep in refrigerator until needed. (See the following directions.)

Chocolate Filling:

1 8-oz pkg. light Philadelphia cream cheese

1 8-oz pkg. fat-free Philadelphia cream cheese

1/2 cup plus 2 Tbsp sugar

1 tsp vanilla

1 egg

1/4 cup fat-free egg substitute

2/3 cup semi-sweet chocolate chips, melted

1 Tbsp creme de cacao liqueur (or similar coffee liqueur)

2 Tbsp cocoa powder

Preheat oven to 350°. Beat all chocolate filling ingredients together until smooth. Pour into prepared chocolate crust. Bake for 30 minutes or until sides are set (center will be soft set). Gently pull out oven rack just enough to reach the inside of the pan. Carefully pour the creamy rum topping in a ring over the outside edge of the chocolate mixture (where the chocolate cheesecake is set). Gently spread the topping evenly over the entire cheesecake. Bake cheesecake for 20 minutes more or until center appears nearly set when gently shaken. Turn off oven and leave cheesecake in oven for 30 minutes. Remove from oven. Once cheesecake has cooled completely, cover and chill in refrigerator for at least 3 hours before serving. Leftovers can be stored in the refrigerator for up to 3 days. Makes 12 servings.

Nutritional analysis per serving:

Calories 312, Fiber 1.2 gm, Cholesterol 50 mg, Sodium 428 mg

% calories from:

Protein 13%, Carbohydrate 52%, Fat 35% (12.5 gm fat)

Less-Fat Caramels

Rich and wonderful homemade caramels can be yours. These caramels take at least 20 minutes of stirring, but you will be rewarded. Plus, they have 75% less butter than traditional caramels.

1 14-oz can low-fat sweetened condensed milk

1/2 cup granulated sugar

1 cup brown sugar

1 1/4 cups light corn syrup

1 cup low-fat milk

4 Tbsp butter

4 tsp vanilla

No-stick cooking spray

Combine all ingredients except vanilla in a nonstick medium saucepan. Bring to a gentle boil and continue to cook, stirring frequently, until it reaches the firm boil stage (248°). This takes a while (20 minutes or so). Remove saucepan from heat and stir in vanilla. Pour into a 9" baking pan lined with foil and coated with no-stick cooking spray. Cool to room temperature and store in refrigerator. Once firm, you can pull the foil liner out from the pan and cut the caramels into 81 pieces (make 9 rows up and down and 9 rows going across (9 x 9 = 81 pieces).

Nutritional analysis per piece:

Calories 50, Cholesterol 2.5 mg, Sodium 16 mg

% calories from:

Protein 3%, Carbohydrate 82%, Fat 15% (0.9 gm fat)

100

Light Breakfasts

Light Denver Omelette for Two

1 cup sliced fresh mushrooms

1 medium green pepper, chopped

4 green onions, sliced diagonally

1/4 tsp dried basil, crushed

1/2 cup low-sodium chicken broth (water can also
be used)

1/2 cup very lean ham cut into 1-inch-long strips
(about 2-3 oz)

1/2 cup cherry tomatoes, halved

1/2 cup fat-free egg substitute

2 eggs, separated

No-stick cooking spray

For Vegetable-Ham Filling:

Coat a medium nonstick frying pan with no-stick cooking spray, and heat over medium heat. Add sliced mushrooms, green pepper, green onions, and basil. Sauté about 20 seconds, then pour in 1/2 cup chicken broth and cook, stirring frequently, until tender. Stir in ham and cherry tomatoes, and cook about a minute to heat through.

For Omelette:

Blend egg substitute and egg yolks in medium-sized bowl and set aside. With mixer, beat egg whites until stiff. Carefully fold egg whites into egg-yolk mixture. Generously coat a nonstick omelette or small nonstick frying pan with no-stick cooking spray (or use 1/2 teaspoon margarine or butter), and heat over medium-low heat. Spread half of egg mixture in pan. Heat until top looks firm (about 2 minutes). If your pan cooks hotter than normal (as some nonstick pans do), cook over low heat. Flip omelette over to lightly brown other side (about 1 minute). Fill with vegetable-ham filling, and fold as desired. Remove to serving plate. Repeat with remaining egg mixture to make 2 fluffy omelettes.

Serving Suggestion:
Serve each omelette with 2 pieces of whole wheat toast with jam or preserves.

Nutritional analysis per omelette:
Calories 188, Fiber 2 gm, Cholesterol 229 mg, Sodium 690 mg

% calories from:
Protein 47%, Carbohydrate 19%, Fat 34% (7 gm fat)

Nutritional analysis per omelette with 2 pieces of whole wheat toast and jam or preserves:
Calories 388, Fiber 8 gm, Cholesterol 229 mg, Sodium 1,107 mg

% calories from:
Protein 29%, Carbohydrate 48%, Fat 23% (10 gm fat)

103

Caramel Apple Breakfast Tart

6 apples

1/2 cup apple juice

8 sheets fillo dough, defrosted

1/2 recipe Light Caramel Sauce (recipe follows)

1/2 tsp ground cinnamon

1 tsp sugar

No-stick cooking spray

Cut the top and bottom off of apples. Cut each into 6 or 8 horizontal slices (so the apple slices are circles). Carve out center where seeds are (will look like donut shape). Place apple slices and apple juice in microwave-safe covered dish, and cook on high for 8 to 10 minutes or until apples are tender; lift from dish with slotted spoon, and set aside to cool. Prepare caramel sauce (next page), and set aside to cool.

Preheat oven to 400°. Coat a 9 x 9 x 2" baking pan with no-stick cooking spray. Place 4 sheets of fillo on top of each other and spray top with no-stick cooking spray. Fold sheets over lengthwise. Place half of the folded fillo in prepared pan. (The remaining half should temporarily lay over one side of the pan.) Spread half of drained apple slices evenly over fillo in pan. Top with 1/2 cup of the caramel sauce. Fold fillo that is outside pan over apple filling. Repeat with 4 more sheets of fillo, remaining apple slices, and caramel sauce. Sprinkle a mixture of ground cinnamon and sugar over the top of fillo. Bake for 15 to 20 minutes or until fillo crust is lightly browned. Makes 9 servings.

Nutritional analysis per serving:

Calories 236, Fiber 3.4 gm, Cholesterol 4 mg, Sodium 155 mg

% calories from:

Protein 5%, Carbohydrate 87%, Fat 8% (2.2 gm fat)

Light Caramel Sauce:

This recipe will work using 2% low-fat milk, but the color and consistency is more appealing using whole milk.

1 Tbsp butter or 2 Tbsp diet margarine

3 Tbsp all-purpose flour

1 1/2 cups whole milk, divided

3/4 cup packed light or dark brown sugar

3/4 cup granulated sugar

1/4 tsp salt

Melt butter in nonstick 2-quart saucepan over medium-low heat; remove from heat. Add 2 tablespoons of the milk, and stir in flour until blended. Return to burner, and gradually stir in remaining milk. Cook, stirring constantly, until the mixture is thickened and smooth. Add brown sugar, sugar, and salt; stir until well mixed. Serve warm, or cover and refrigerate to serve cold. Store any leftovers in the refrigerator. Makes about 2 cups of caramel sauce.

Bacon & Cheese Biscuits

5 strips Louis Rich turkey bacon (or similar)

2 cups all-purpose flour

1 Tbsp baking powder

2 tsp sugar

1/2 tsp cream of tartar

1/4 tsp salt

1/4 tsp baking soda

1/4 cup butter-flavored shortening (butter or margarine can also be used)

1/4 cup fat-free cream cheese

2-3 oz reduced-fat sharp cheddar cheese, grated (1/2 cup very firmly packed)

2/3 cup low-fat buttermilk

No-stick cooking spray

Preheat oven to 350°. Fry bacon strips over medium-low heat, turning frequently until crisp. Let cool, then crumble into tiny bits. In mixing bowl, stir together next six ingredients. Using a pastry blender, cut in shortening and cream cheese until mixture resembles coarse crumbs. Stir in bacon bits and grated cheese. Make a well in the center, and add buttermilk all at once. Stir with fork just until moistened. Turn dough onto lightly floured surface, and knead gently (fold and press dough about 10 times). Pat or roll dough to 1/2" thickness. Using 2 1/2" biscuit cutter, cut dough into biscuits. Place on baking sheet coated

lightly with no-stick cooking spray. Bake for 10 minutes
or until biscuits are done. Makes 10 large biscuits.

Nutritional analysis per biscuit:

Calories 182, Fiber 1 gm, Cholesterol 9 mg, Sodium 315 mg

% calories from:

Protein 13%, Carbohydrate 47%, Fat 40% (8 gm fat)

Apple Butter Mini Spice Cakes

If you prefer to use oil instead of shortening, use 2 tablespoons of oil and increase the apple butter to 6 tablespoons. The cakes will come out fine, but the oil batter doesn't whip up as nice and fluffy. You can also use all-purpose flour instead of cake flour, but the crumb won't be quite as tender.

   3 Tbsp butter-flavored shortening (regular can be
      substituted)
   5 Tbsp apple butter (you can find it in jars in the
      jam/preserve section of most supermarkets)
   1 egg
   1/4 cup fat-free egg substitute
   1 cup packed dark brown sugar
   3/4 cup low-fat buttermilk
   1 tsp vanilla
   2 cups cake flour (all-purpose flour can be substituted)
   1 tsp baking soda
   1 tsp baking powder
   1 tsp salt
   1 tsp ground cinnamon
   1 tsp ground allspice
   1/2 tsp ground cloves
   1/2 tsp ground nutmeg
   1/4 cup chopped nuts (optional)
   1/2 recipe Maple Glaze (optional), recipe follows

Preheat oven to 350°. Coat a 12-muffin tin generously with no-stick cooking spray.

In large mixing bowl, beat shortening, apple butter, and the egg together briefly. Add in egg substitute, brown sugar, buttermilk, and vanilla, and beat at low speed until blended. In medium sized bowl, mix flour, baking soda, baking powder, salt, cinnamon, allspice, cloves, and nutmeg together. Add to apple butter mixture on low speed until blended. Beat at high speed for 3 minutes.

Ladle batter into muffin cups, filling each cup to about 1/4" from the top. Bake for about 15 minutes or until muffins spring back when you press the center with your finger. Let cool, then frost each with a little maple glaze; sprinkle chopped nuts over the glaze if desired. Makes 12 servings.

Nutritional analysis per serving:
Calories 191, Fiber 0.6 gm, Cholesterol 18 mg, Sodium 310 mg

% calories from:
Protein 6%, Carbohydrate 75%, Fat 19% (4 gm fat)

Maple Glaze:

2 Tbsp brown sugar

1 Tbsp butter

5 Tbsp milk (low-fat can be used)

At least 1 cup powdered sugar

Combine brown sugar, butter, and milk in small nonstick saucepan, and heat until butter melts. Remove from heat and stir in powdered sugar until thick and of spreading consistency.

Egg Muffin Lite

To lower the cholesterol even further, use 1/2 cup fat-free egg sub-stitute instead of 1 egg and 1/4 cup egg substitute, but it won't taste quite as authentic.

> 2 English muffins, toasted
>
> 1 egg
>
> 1/4 cup fat-free egg substitute
>
> 2 slices Canadian bacon
>
> 2 6 1/2-oz empty tuna cans (or similar), washed, with label removed
>
> Freshly ground pepper
>
> 2 slices 1/3 less fat American cheese slices
>
> No-stick cooking spray

Coat half of a 9 or 10" nonstick frying pan with no-stick cooking spray, and heat over medium heat. In small bowl, beat the egg with egg substitute; set aside. Place Canadian bacon in the pan over the spray coated area. Spray inside of the tuna can with no-stick cooking spray, and set can on the other side of the pan to start heating. When bottom side of the bacon is light brown, flip over to the other side and cook until light brown. Remove slices from pan and set aside.

Pour half of egg mixture (1/4 cup) into tuna can. Sprinkle with freshly ground pepper to taste. When the surface of egg begins to firm, cut around the inside of the can with a butter knife to free the edges. Turn the egg over with a cake fork, and cook for 1 minute more. Remove egg from can. Coat can with no-stick cooking spray. Repeat with remaining egg.

To assemble Egg Muffin Lites, layer English muffin bottom with a slice of cheese, then egg, a piece of Canadian bacon, and the English muffin top half. To reheat, microwave each sandwich for 20 seconds on high. Makes 2 sandwiches.

Nutritional analysis per serving:

Calories 287, Fiber 1.5 gm, Cholesterol 130 mg, Sodium 1,157 mg

% calories from:

Protein 30%, Carbohydrate 43%, Fat 27% (8.6 gm fat)

Zucchini-Tomato Frittata

3 eggs
3/4 cup fat-free egg substitute
1/8 tsp pepper
1 cup thinly sliced or diced zucchini
1/2 cup chopped onion
1-2 cloves garlic, minced
1/4 cup water or chicken or beef broth
1 cup chopped tomato
3 Tbsp grated Parmesan or Romano cheese
No-stick cooking spray

In mixer bowl, beat eggs with egg substitute and pepper; set aside. Microwave zucchini with 1/4 cup of water in microwave-safe dish covered until tender; drain and set aside. Coat a nonstick 10" skillet with no-stick cooking spray. Add onion, garlic, and water or broth, and cook over medium heat until tender. Stir in zucchini and tomato. Spread evenly in skillet. Pour egg mixture into skillet. As mixture sets, run a spatula around the edge of skillet, lifting egg mixture to allow uncooked portions to flow underneath. Continue cooking until almost set. Remove from heat; cover and let stand 4 minutes or until top is set. Sprinkle with Parmesan cheese. Cut into wedges. Makes 4 servings.

Serving Suggestion:

Serve each wedge with a roll or slice of bread. Frittata can also be served over a thin bed of steamed rice.

Nutritional analysis per serving (including bread):

Calories 261, Fiber 2 gm, Cholesterol 218 mg, Sodium 499 mg

% calories from:

Protein 31%, Carbohydrate 40%, Fat 29% (8 gm fat)

Bagel & Egg Sandwich

1 egg

1/4 cup fat-free egg substitute

About 1/4 tsp mixed dried herbs, if desired (e.g., Italian herb seasoning)

2 slices 1/3 less fat American cheese or 1/2 cup grated reduced-fat sharp cheddar cheese

2 bagels, sliced, and toasted if desired

No-stick cooking spray

Beat egg together with egg substitute. Add herbs if desired. Coat a nonstick 9 or 10" frying pan with no-stick cooking spray, and heat over medium heat. Pour in egg mixture. Cook until bottom side is light brown, loosening egg from side of pan so any loose egg mixture can drip to the bottom of pan. Flip over and cook other side until light browned. Remove from heat and cut in half and fold each half over. Lay one slice of cheese on each half, then fold each half over. Place each cheese and egg serving in between two bagel slices. Makes two sandwiches.

NOTE: You can also follow directions for making a perfectly round egg in the Egg Muffin Lite recipe on page 110.

Nutritional analysis per serving:

Calories 194, Fiber 0.6 gm, Cholesterol 116 mg, Sodium 566 mg

% calories from:

Protein 31%, Carbohydrate 41%, Fat 28% (6 gm fat)

Whole Wheat Cinnamon Toast

This is one of my favorite and quickest breakfasts. It's wonderful with raisin bread or cinnamon swirl bread, too. I always have a mixture of cinnamon and sugar ready for a quick batch of cinnamon toast.

1 1/2 tsp granulated sugar

1/4 tsp ground cinnamon

2 slices whole wheat bread

2 tsp diet margarine (or 1 1/2 tsp butter or stick margarine, softened)

In small bowl or cup, blend sugar with cinnamon; set aside. Toast slices of bread. Once they pop up from the toaster, immediately spread each with half the margarine or butter. Sprinkle with cinnamon-sugar mixture to taste. Makes 1 serving.

Nutritional analysis per serving:

Calories 237, Fiber 5.6 gm, Cholesterol 0, Sodium 512 mg

% calories from:

Protein 11%, Carbohydrate 57%, Fat 32% (8.7 gm fat)

Serving Suggestion:

For a more complete meal, serve with fresh fruit and a glass of skim milk.

Chocolate Zucchini Muffins

I know pairing chocolate with zucchini sounds like an unlikely partnership — but hey, don't knock it till you've tried it. This recipe comes in real handy when you've got 4 large zucchinis you're trying to use up, and you're on your fourth loaf of zucchini bread.

1 egg

6 Tbsp fat-free egg substitute

1 cup sugar

2 tsp vanilla

3 Tbsp vegetable oil

5 Tbsp chocolate syrup

2 cups unsifted flour

1/3 cup cocoa

1 tsp baking powder

1 tsp baking soda

1 tsp ground cinnamon

1/2 tsp salt

3/4 cup low-fat buttermilk

2 cups firmly packed grated zucchini

1/3 cup semi-sweet chocolate chips (optional)

No-stick cooking spray

Preheat oven to 350°. Coat about 16 muffin cups generously with no-stick cooking spray, or spray the inside of about 20 muffin cup liners with no-stick cooking spray. In large mixing bowl, beat egg and egg substitute on high until light and fluffy. Gradually beat in sugar and vanilla until thick and light in color. Add oil and chocolate syrup and beat well.

In separate bowl, combine flour with cocoa, baking powder, baking soda, cinnamon, and salt. Add to batter alternately with buttermilk, beginning and ending with the flour mixture. Fold in zucchini and chocolate chips (if desired). Spoon about 1/3 cup of muffin batter into each prepared muffin cup, or spoon about 1/4 cup of batter into each paper liner. Bake for 25 minutes for the 20 smaller muffins or 30 minutes for the 16 larger muffins.

Nutritional analysis per muffin:

Calories 160, Fiber 1.3 gm, Cholesterol 14 mg, Sodium 184 mg

% calories from:

Protein 9%, Carbohydrate 72%, Fat 19% (3.5 gm fat) — If adding the chocolate chips, each muffin will contain 178 calories and 23% calories from fat (4.8 gm fat) if 16 muffins per batch.

Raspberry Whole Wheat Muffins

1 egg

1/8 cup fat-free egg substitute (or 1 egg white)

2 Tbsp vegetable oil

1/4 cup molasses

1/4 cup brown sugar, packed

3/4 cup low-fat buttermilk

1 tsp vanilla

3/4 cup quick or old-fashioned oats

1 3/4 cups whole wheat flour

1 tsp baking powder

1 1/2 tsp baking soda

1 tsp ground cinnamon

11 Tbsp less-sugar raspberry jam (or similar)

No-stick cooking spray

Preheat oven to 375°. Coat muffin tin with no-stick cooking spray. Combine egg, egg substitute, oil, molasses, brown sugar, buttermilk, vanilla, and oats, and let soak for 10 minutes.

In separate bowl, combine dry ingredients. Pour dry ingredients into wet ingredients and mix well. Spoon batter into 11 muffin cups. Make a dent with a spoon (or thumb) in the middle of each muffin. Spoon one tablespoon jelly into the middle of each muffin. Bake 18 to 20 minutes. Makes 11 muffins.

Nutritional analysis per muffin:

Calories 216, Fiber 3.5 gm, Cholesterol 20 mg, Sodium 182 mg

% calories from:

Protein 9%, Carbohydrate 76%, Fat 15% (3.8 gm fat)

Cranberry-Oat Orange Bread

2 cups all-purpose flour

1 cup quick or old fashioned oats

3/4 cup sugar

2 tsp baking powder

1/2 tsp baking soda

1/2 tsp salt (optional)

1/2 cup light sour cream

1/4 cup orange juice concentrate

1 egg

1/4 cup fat-free egg substitute

2 Tbsp vegetable oil

1 Tbsp grated orange peel (orange zest)

1 cup chopped cranberries

1/4 cup nuts (optional)

No-stick cooking spray

120

Preheat oven to 350°. Coat 9 x 5" loaf pan with no-stick cooking spray. Combine flour, oats, sugar, baking powder, baking soda, and salt if desired, mixing well; set aside. Beat sour cream, orange juice concentrate, egg, egg substitute, oil, and orange peel until mixed thoroughly. Add to dry ingredients, mixing just until moistened. Stir in cranberries and nuts. Pour into prepared pan. Bake 55 to 60 minutes or until fork inserted in center comes out clean. Cool 10 minutes then remove from pan to cool completely. Makes 12 slices.

Nutritional analysis per slice:

Calories 199, Fiber 2 gm, Cholesterol 19 mg, Sodium 109 mg

% calories from:

Protein 10%, Carbohydrate 74%, Fat 16% (3.6 gm fat)

Peanut Butter Pancakes

My four-year-old daughter, Devon, thought these up one morning. She likes to eat them with grape jelly spread on top.

1/4 cup reduced-fat peanut butter
1/4 cup fat-free egg substitute
1/2 cup plus 2 Tbsp skim or low-fat milk
1 cup reduced-fat Bisquick
No-stick cooking spray

Beat peanut butter with egg substitute. Add in milk and beat until smooth. Stir in Bisquick mix until blended. Coat a nonstick frying pan generously with no-stick cooking spray, and heat over low heat. Pour pancake batter into pan, about 1/4 cup of batter per pancake. Cook until bottom is browned, then flip over and cook until second side is nicely browned. Remove from pan. Repeat previous steps until all pancakes are cooked. Makes 3 servings.

121

Nutritional analysis:
Calories 302, Fiber 2 gm, Cholesterol 1 mg, Sodium 685 mg

% calories from:
Protein 16%, Carbohydrate 53%, Fat 31% (10.5 gm fat)

Lemon Scones

These scones go great with strawberry or raspberry jam. They're so rich tasting and moist, you'll never know the butter was reduced from the original 10 tablespoons.

3 cups flour

6 Tbsp sugar

2 Tbsp plus 2 tsp baking powder

1/4 cup butter, softened

1/4 cup plus 2 Tbsp fat-free cream cheese

Zest from 1 lemon, finely chopped (lemon peel removed with zesting tool)

1 6-oz container low-fat lemon yogurt

1/2 cup plus 1 Tbsp 1% or 2% low-fat milk

No-stick cooking spray

Preheat oven to 325°. Mix flour, sugar, and baking powder in medium bowl. With mixer or food processor, blend butter, cream cheese, and lemon zest until smooth. Cut this mixture into flour mixture to get a coarse-meal consistency. Use mixer to beat yogurt with milk until smooth. Stir this into the flour mixture. Turn out on floured board and pat until it holds together, handling as little as possible. Press dough into a rectangle about 6 x 11" and a little over 1/2" thick. Cut rectangle in half from top to bottom and from side to side. Cut each of these smaller rectangles diagonally to make 8 triangles altogether. Place on cookie sheet coated with no-stick cooking spray (or use nonstick cookie sheet). Bake for 25 to 30 minutes or until nicely browned. Makes 8 large scones.

NOTE: You can brush the tops with a glaze made from 4 teaspoons lemon juice and 2/3 cup powdered sugar.

Nutritional analysis per scone:

Calories 303, Fiber 1.3 gm, Cholesterol 18 mg, Sodium 476 mg

% calories from:

Protein 11%, Carbohydrate 70%, Fat 19% (6.5 gm fat)

Strawberry-Filled French Toast

*I thought of this recipe after making a wonderful batch of home-
made strawberry jam and trying to find ways to use it. This is a
nice and easy variation on the traditional French toast.*

> 4 1-inch slices French bread (or 8 thin slices of any type
>   of bread)
>
> 1/4 cup strawberry jam
>
> 1 egg
>
> 1/4 cup fat-free egg substitute
>
> 1/2 cup low-fat milk
>
> No-stick cooking spray

Make a pocket in each thick slice of bread, cutting almost
in half lengthwise. Spread about 1 tablespoon of jam in
each pocket. (If using thin slices of bread, spread the jam
on one of the slices and top with another slice of bread.)
Set slices aside.

In mixing bowl, beat egg, egg substitute and milk together until well blended. Pour into an 8 x 8 x 2" baking pan
(or similar size pan.) Coat a nonstick frying pan generously with no-stick cooking spray, then heat over medium
low heat. Place one of the slices in the egg mixture. After
about 5 seconds, flip the slice over to coat the other side
with egg. After 5 seconds, lift from the pan and let drip for
a few seconds, then place in frying pan. Spray top of the
French toast with no-stick cooking spray. Let cook until
bottom is lightly browned. Flip slice over, and brown the
second side. Repeat steps with the other slices (if using
thin slices, just proceed as if the two thin slices with jam

in the middle were one thick slice). Makes 4 small servings.

Nutritional analysis per serving:

Calories 285, Fiber 1.3 gm, Cholesterol 57 mg, Sodium 467 mg

% calories from:

Protein 15%, Carbohydrate 72%, Fat 13% (4 gm fat)

Sock-It-to-Me Coffee Cake

I know at 10 grams of fat a slice this coffee cake seems more like a dessert than a breakfast, but there are times when you may want a quick-fix coffee cake recipe. And this one is a winner.

1 package Duncan Hines Moist Deluxe Butter Recipe golden cake mix, divided

2 Tbsp brown sugar

2 tsp ground cinnamon

1/2 cup finely chopped pecans

1/3 cup flaked coconut

1/2 cup fat-free egg substitute

1 egg

2/3 cup fat-free or light sour cream

2/3 cup unsweetened chunky applesauce

1/4 cup apple juice or water

No-stick cooking spray

Glaze:

1 cup confectioners' sugar

1 to 2 Tbsp milk

Preheat oven to 375°. Coat 10" tube pan with no-stick cooking spray. For streusel filling, combine 2 tablespoons dry cake mix, brown sugar, and cinnamon in small bowl. Stir in pecans and coconut. Set aside.

For cake, combine remaining cake mix, egg substitute, egg, sour cream, applesauce, and apple juice in a large bowl. Beat at medium speed with electric mixer for 2 minutes. Pour two-thirds of batter into pan. Sprinkle evenly with streusel filling. Spoon remaining batter evenly over filling. Bake for 45 to 55 minutes or until toothpick inserted in center comes out clean. Cool in pan 30 minutes. Invert onto serving plate to cool completely.

For glaze, combine confectioners' sugar and milk in small bowl. Stir until smooth. Drizzle over cake. Makes 10 servings.

Nutritional analysis per serving:

Calories 359, Fiber 3 gm, Cholesterol 21 mg, Sodium 237 mg

% calories from:

Protein 7%, Carbohydrate 68%, Fat 25% (10 gm fat)

Bacon & Cheese Muffins

2 cups all-purpose flour

2 Tbsp baking powder

1/2 tsp salt

2 Tbsp softened butter

2 Tbsp maple syrup or pancake syrup

1/4 cup fat-free cream cheese

1/4 cup sugar

1 egg

1/4 cup fat-free egg substitute

1 cup 1% low-fat milk (or similar)

1 cup grated reduced-fat sharp cheddar cheese
(about 4 oz)

6 strips crisp cooked Louis Rich less-fat turkey bacon,
crumbled into pieces

1 tsp dried basil (optional)

No-stick cooking spray

Preheat oven to 350°. Coat muffin tin generously with no-stick cooking spray.

Blend flour, baking powder, and salt in medium bowl. In another bowl, cream together butter, maple syrup, and cream cheese. Add sugar and blend until smooth. Add egg and egg substitute and beat well. Add about a third of the dry ingredients and blend; then add about a third of the milk and blend. Repeat with remaining flour mixture and milk until both are blended into the batter. Quickly fold in cheese, bacon pieces, and basil. Scoop batter into prepared muffin tins using a 1/4 cup measure, slightly heaping with batter. Bake in center of oven until light brown

on top and cooked throughout, about 25 minutes. Makes
12 muffins.

Nutritional analysis per muffin:

Calories 184, Fiber 0.6 gm, Cholesterol 34.5 mg, Sodium 458 mg

% calories from:

Protein 19%, Carbohydrate 54%, Fat 27% (5.5 gm fat)

Banana Rum Raisin Bread

1 1/4 cups plus 2 Tbsp all-purpose or unbleached flour

1/2 cup whole wheat flour

1 cup sugar

2 tsp baking powder

1 tsp salt

1 1/2 cups (3 medium) mashed ripe bananas

2 Tbsp canola oil (or butter or margarine, softened)

1/4 cup dark rum

2 Tbsp molasses

1 egg

1/4 to 1/2 cup raisins (or pecans or walnuts)

Rum glaze (optional)

No-stick cooking spray

Rum Glaze:

Mix 1 cup powdered sugar with 2 teaspoons dark rum and 2 teaspoons apple juice in small bowl until smooth. Set aside until needed.

Preheat oven to 350°. Coat a 9 x 5" or 8 x 4" loaf pan with no-stick cooking spray. Dust pan lightly with flour. Lightly spoon flour into measuring cup. In mixing bowl, add flours, sugar, baking powder, salt, bananas, oil, rum, molasses, and egg. Beat for 3 minutes at medium speed. Stir in raisins. Pour batter into prepared loaf pan. Bake in center of oven for 55 to 60 minutes or until toothpick inserted in center comes out clean. Cool 10 minutes then remove from pan to finish cooling. Spoon glaze over top if desired. Makes 8 thick slices (or 12 thin slices).

Nutritional analysis per thick slice:

Calories 299, Fiber 2.5 gm, Cholesterol 34 mg, Sodium 388 mg

% calories from:

Protein 6%, Carbohydrate 82%, Fat 12% (4 gm fat)

Oil-Free Potato Pancakes

These hearty pancakes are great for breakfast or as a part of lunch or dinner. Serve them hot with applesauce or catsup.

4 medium sized raw potatoes, peeled and grated

1 onion, grated

2 eggs, separated

1/2 tsp salt

1/4 tsp freshly ground pepper

2 Tbsp all-purpose flour

No-stick cooking spray

In medium sized bowl, toss the potatoes with the onions. Beat the egg yolks and add them to the potato mixture. Blend in salt, pepper, and flour. With mixer, beat the egg whites until stiff peaks form. Gently fold them into the potato mixture. Spray a high quality, nonstick frying pan with cooking spray, then heat it over medium-low heat. (If you don't have a high quality, nonstick frying pan, use the frying pan you have and lightly grease it with butter or oil—about 1 tablespoon for entire recipe—before frying each batch of pancakes.)

Drop batter by large tablespoonfuls onto the pan. Spray the top of the pancakes with cooking spray. When the bottoms are brown, flip pancakes over. Remove from pan when the second side is brown. Repeat until all the batter is used. Makes about 6 servings or about 20 potato pancakes.

Nutritional analysis per serving:

Calories 141, Fiber 2 gm, Cholesterol 71 mg, Sodium 205 mg

% calories from:

Protein 13%, Carbohydrate 75%, Fat 12% (1.8 gm fat)

Sun-Dried Tomato-Pesto Bagel Spread

1/2 cup light or fat-free cream cheese

1 clove garlic, minced or pressed

2 tsp basil leaves, bottled in water, fresh/chopped, or dried soaked in warm water

2 Tbsp julienne-style sun-dried tomatoes from bag, soaked in warm water until tender, then drained

1 to 2 Tbsp roasted nuts (pine nuts, pecans, or walnuts)

Add all ingredients to food processor and process until well blended. Makes spread for about 3 bagels.

Nutritional analysis per serving of spread with bagel (using light cream cheese):

Calories 299, Fiber 2 gm, Cholesterol 20 mg, Sodium 504 mg

% calories from:

Protein 19%, Carbohydrate 54%, Fat 27% (9 gm fat)

Nutritional analysis per serving of spread only (using light cream cheese):

Calories 119, Fiber 0.8 gm, Cholesterol 20 mg, Sodium 204 mg

% calories from:

Protein 18%, Carbohydrate 21%, Fat 61% (8 gm fat)

Herb & Onion Bagel Spread

1 small onion, peeled and cut into about 10 slices

4 oz light or fat-free cream cheese

1 Tbsp fresh chives, finely chopped

1 1/2 tsp fresh basil, finely chopped (if using bottled basil, use 1 tsp)

No-stick cooking spray

Coat a sheet of foil (about 9 x 13") generously with no-stick cooking spray. Lay onion slices evenly over foil. Spray onions with no-stick cooking spray. Broil until top is light brown, watching carefully. Flip onion slices over and let second side brown. Remove from heat. Let cool.

In small food processor blend all ingredients until smooth. If you don't have a small food processor, finely chop the onion slices and blend all the ingredients together well with mixer. Makes about 1/2 cup of spread.

135

Nutritional analysis per 1/8 cup of spread with bagel (using light cream cheese):

Calories 262, Fiber 2 gm, Cholesterol 15 mg, Sodium 450 mg

% calories from:

Protein 18%, Carbohydrate 61%, Fat 21% (6 gm fat)

Nutritional analysis per 1/8 cup of spread only (using light cream cheese):

Calories 82, Fiber 0.5 gm, Cholesterol 15 mg, Sodium 151 mg

% calories from:

Protein 18%, Carbohydrate 26%, Fat 56% (5 gm fat)

Lox-Ness Monster Bagel Spread

1/2 cup light cream cheese (you can also use fat-free or a
combination of light and fat-free if you desire)

2 oz lox, finely chopped

1 green onion, finely chopped (optional)

Blend all ingredients in food processor until well mixed.
You should still be able to see some small pieces of lox.
Makes about 4 servings of spread.

Nutritional analysis per 2 Tbsp of spread with bagel:

Calories 267, Fiber 1 gm, Cholesterol 18 mg, Sodium 561 mg

% calories from:

Protein 20%, Carbohydrate 57%, Fat 22% (6.6 gm fat)

Lemon Zucchini Muffins

2 cups all-purpose flour

1/2 cup sugar

1 Tbsp baking powder

1 tsp salt

Grated peel of 1/2 large lemon (or 1 small lemon)

1/3 cup chopped walnuts (optional)

1 egg, beaten

1/4 cup fat-free egg substitute

1/2 cup low-fat buttermilk

2 Tbsp vegetable oil

2 Tbsp lemon juice

2 Tbsp cup low-fat lemon yogurt (vanilla yogurt or light sour cream can also be used)

1 cup (packed) shredded zucchini

No-stick cooking spray

Preheat oven to 400°. Combine flour, sugar, baking powder, salt, and lemon peel in a large bowl. Stir in walnuts if desired. In a smaller bowl, combine egg, egg substitute, buttermilk, oil, lemon juice, and lemon yogurt. Make a well in center of dry ingredients and add the wet ingredients. Stir just until combined and gently fold in zucchini. Spoon batter into a 12-cup muffin tin coated with no-stick cooking spray. Bake for 20 to 25 minutes or until muffins spring back when gently pressed. Makes 10 to 12 muffins.

Nutritional analysis per muffin (if 12 per recipe):

Calories 147, Fiber 1 gm, Cholesterol 18 mg, Sodium 287 mg

% calories from:

Protein 10%, Carbohydrate 71%, Fat 19% (3 gm fat)

Apple Lover's Oatmeal

1 packet instant oatmeal, plain
1 individual cup applesauce (3.9 oz), unsweetened
   (or 1/3 cup)
2 Tbsp brown sugar
1/4 tsp ground cinnamon
1/2 cup low-fat milk, skim milk, or water

In large microwave-safe soup bowl, blend all ingredients together. Microwave on high for 1 1/2 minutes. Stir, then microwave for another 1 1/2 minutes. Serve hot. Makes 1 serving.

Nutritional analysis per serving:
Calories 225, Fiber 2.3 gm, Cholesterol 5 mg, Sodium 140 mg

% calories from:
Protein 10%, Carbohydrate 84%, Fat 6% (1.6 gm fat)

Vegetable Scramble

Whip this up in the morning and have it with a toasted bagel, slices of whole wheat bread, or oil-free hashbrowns or potatoes.

1 egg or 1/4 cup egg substitute

2 Tbsp milk (skim, low-fat, or other)

1/2 cup assorted finely chopped vegetables (at least two different vegetables — zucchini, onion, bell pepper, broccoli, tomato — whatever you have)

Herbs as desired (I like to add a pinch of oregano or sage and a pinch of pepper)

Sprinkle of Parmesan or grated reduced-fat cheese (optional)

No-stick cooking spray

Stir the egg and milk together. Coat an omelette sized non-stick pan with no-stick cooking spray. Heat over medium-low heat. Add vegetables and cook, stirring frequently, for a couple minutes. Add egg mixture and herbs, and cook, stirring frequently until egg is desired doneness. Sprinkle with cheese if desired. Makes 1 serving.

Nutritional analysis per serving (egg scramble only—not including toast or potatoes):

Calories 107, Fiber 1 gm, Cholesterol 213 mg, Sodium 81 mg

% calories from:

Protein 30%, Carbohydrate 25%, Fat 45% (5 gm fat)

139

Light Lunches

Mexican-Style Potato

1 baked potato (pierce with fork, then cook in microwave on high until tender—about 5 to 8 minutes)

1/8 cup salsa

1 green onion, chopped

1/4 cup fat-free refried beans or canned pinto, kidney, or pinquito beans

1 oz reduced-fat Monterey Jack cheese (or reduced-fat cheddar), grated (about 1/4 cup)

Split potato in half and loosen filling by pressing down on potato with fork. Spread salsa over open potato. In small bowl, blend green onion with beans and cheese. Spread onto potato. Microwave on high about 3 minutes or until cheese melts. Makes 1 serving.

Nutritional analysis per serving:

Calories 371, Fiber 10 gm, Cholesterol 15 mg, Sodium 194 mg

% calories from:

Protein 18%, Carbohydrate 69%, Fat 14% (6 gm fat)

Pizza Potato

1 baked potato (pierce with fork, then cook in microwave on high until tender—about 5 to 8 minutes)

1/8 cup bottled marinara or spaghetti sauce (with 4 gm fat per 4-oz serving)

1 clove garlic, minced or pressed

1 green onion, chopped

1 oz part-skim mozzarella cheese, grated (about 1/4 cup)

1 Tbsp Parmesan cheese

1/2 tsp Italian herb seasoning (optional)

Split potato in half and loosen filling by pressing down on potato with fork. Blend marinara sauce with crushed garlic; spread over open potato. In small bowl, blend green onion with cheeses and Italian herbs. Sprinkle onto potato. Microwave on high about 3 minutes or until cheese melts. Makes 1 serving.

Nutritional analysis per serving:

Calories 352, Fiber 5 gm, Cholesterol 20 mg, Sodium 395 mg

% calories from:

Protein 18%, Carbohydrate 62%, Fat 20% (8 gm fat)

143

Quick-Fix Fried Rice

1 Tbsp diet margarine (e.g., light I Can't Believe It's Not Butter)

1 container Kan Tong Fried Rice (from Uncle Ben's—it comes in several flavors and is packaged in a Chinese take-out box)

1 3/4 cups low-sodium chicken or beef broth (or water)

1/2 cup fat-free egg substitute

Low-sodium soy sauce to taste

No-stick cooking spray

Coat a large frying pan or skillet (with cover) generously with no-stick cooking spray. Heat over medium heat. Add margarine and rice, and sauté for 2 minutes, stirring constantly. Add broth or water and contents of the seasoning packet that comes with the rice; bring to boil.

Cover pan and reduce heat to medium-low. Simmer 18 minutes or until rice is tender. For best results, don't open lid while simmering.

While rice is simmering, make your omelettes to garnish the rice: Coat a small frying pan generously with no-stick cooking spray. Heat pan over medium heat. Pour 2 tablespoons of the egg substitute into pan, and tilt pan to cover bottom of pan. When bottom side is lightly browned, flip to other side. When both sides are done, remove from pan and set aside. Repeat until all of the egg substitute is gone, making about 4 omelettes. Shred omelettes into bite-sized pieces. When rice is ready, top with omelette pieces and sprinkle with soy sauce. Makes 2 servings.

Nutritional analysis per serving:

Calories 377, Fiber 1.3 gm, Cholesterol 0, Sodium 400 mg (not including soy sauce)

% calories from:

Protein 19%, Carbohydrate 69%, Fat 12% (5 gm fat)

The 3-Minute Burrito

1/2 cup cooked or canned pinto beans or pinquitos (small brown beans), drained and rinsed

1 Tbsp chopped fresh cilantro (optional)

2 Tbsp light sour cream

1 green onion, chopped

1/8 cup chunky salsa (mild or hot depending on preference)

1 burrito size flour tortilla

1 1/2 oz reduced-fat Monterey Jack or sharp cheddar cheese, grated (about a heaping 1/3 cup)

In small bowl, toss beans, cilantro, sour cream, green onion, and salsa together. Heat tortilla in microwave on a double thickness of paper towel for about 1 minute or until soft. Sprinkle cheese evenly over the tortilla. Spread bean mixture in center of tortilla. Fold bottom and top ends of tortilla in and roll up into a burrito. Microwave 1 more minute or until burrito is heated through. Makes 1 serving.

Nutritional analysis per serving:

Calories 433, Fiber 12 gm, Cholesterol 26 mg, Sodium 481 mg

% calories from:

Protein 22%, Carbohydrate 50%, Fat 28% (14 gm fat)

3-Minute Microwave Chili Dog

4, 50% less fat hot dogs (e.g., Louis Rich turkey franks)
4 hot dog buns
1 15-oz can Hormel fat-free vegetarian chili (or similar)
1/2 cup grated reduced-fat sharp cheddar cheese

Place each hot dog in a bun on a microwave-safe plate.
Place hot dog in bun. Spoon about 1/2 cup of chili over
each hot dog. Sprinkle cheese over chili. Microwave each
chili dog on high for approximately 3 minutes or until
heated through and cheese has melted. Makes 4 servings.

NOTE: This chili dog should be the only high-sodium
meal eaten this day since it contains over half of the sodium recommended for a day.

Nutritional analysis per serving:

Calories 400, Fiber 5.5 gm, Cholesterol 60 mg, Sodium 1,465 mg

% calories from:

Protein 21%, Carbohydrate 50%, Fat 29% (13 gm fat)

147

Biscuit Pan Pizza

1 cup reduced-fat Bisquick

1/4 cup low-fat or nonfat milk

Pinch of oregano and basil dry leaves

1 Tbsp grated Parmesan cheese

2 oz part-skim or low-fat mozzarella cheese (1/2 cup grated)

2 green onions

1/3 cup diced zucchini or 1/2 cup thinly sliced zucchini

1/3 cup bottled marinara or spaghetti sauce (with 4 gm fat per 4 oz)

Olive oil no-stick cooking spray

NOTE: Other vegetables can be added instead of or in addition to the zucchini, like red or green pepper (finely chopped) or artichoke hearts, etc.

Preheat oven to 450°. In small bowl, mix Bisquick with milk. Knead a few times to blend in loose crumbs. Coat a 9" pie plate with no-stick cooking spray. Press biscuit dough in pie plate. Spray top with no-stick cooking spray. Sprinkle oregano, basil, and Parmesan cheese over the top. Bake for 8 minutes. While the biscuit crust is baking, grate the mozzarella, and chop the green onions and zucchini or other vegetables.

Toss grated cheese, onions, zucchini, and other vegetables together in medium sized bowl. Spread marinara sauce evenly over the baked crust, and top with the cheese and vegetable mixture. Bake 15 minutes more or until crust is brown and cheese is melted. Makes 2 servings.

148

Nutritional analysis per serving:

Calories 365, Fiber 2 gm, Cholesterol 19 mg, Sodium 1,075 mg

% calories from:

Protein 17%, Carbohydrate 55%, Fat 28% (11 gm fat)

Fish Sandwich

1 light breaded frozen fish fillet (e.g., Van de Kamp's light cod fillet

1 hamburger bun

1 Tbsp Light Tartar Sauce (recipe follows)

Lettuce and tomato, if desired

Preheat oven to 425°. Place fish fillet on a piece of foil and bake 25 minutes until browned (turn after 15 minutes). If you prefer to microwave, place fish fillet on double thickness of paper towels, and cook on high for 3 to 4 minutes for 1 fillet or 5 to 6 minutes for 2 fillets (rotate fish 1/4 turn after 2 minutes). Place fish on foil or baking sheet, and broil 1 minute on each side.

Spread tartar sauce on bottom half of the bun, and top with fish fillet. Add lettuce and tomato if desired. Top with bun. Makes 1 serving.

150

Nutritional analysis per serving:

Calories 380, Fiber 1 gm, Cholesterol 42 mg, Sodium 758 mg

% calories from:

Protein 22%, Carbohydrate 44%, Fat 34% (14.5 gm of fat)
(To lower the % calories from fat for the meal, serve the fish sandwich with a fresh fruit salad)

Light Tartar Sauce:

1/2 cup light mayonnaise

1/2 cup low-fat or nonfat mayonnaise

2 Tbsp minced parsley

2 Tbsp minced dill pickle (or dill pickle relish)

2 Tbsp finely minced onion

1/2 tsp sugar

Pepper to taste

1 Tbsp]capers (optional)

1 Tbsp minced pimento-stuffed olives (optional)

In small bowl, stir above ingredients together until well blended. Makes more than a cup.

Quick-Fix Chili and Fries

12 oz low-fat frozen French fries (e.g., Ore Ida Potato Wedges), approximately 3 1/2 cups

2 oz reduced-fat sharp cheddar cheese, grated (1/2 cup firmly packed)

1 15-oz can fat-free Hormel vegetarian chili (or similar)

Preheat oven to 450°. Arrange frozen french fries in a single layer on baking sheet or shallow pan. Bake 20 to 25 minutes, turning after 15 minutes, or until desired crispness and color. Spoon chili into two serving bowls. Heat in microwave (about 3 minutes for each bowl on high) or place in a small casserole dish; heat in oven along with the French fries. Sprinkle grated cheese over the chili before serving. Serve with fries on the side. Makes 2 servings.

Nutritional analysis per serving:

Calories 500, Fiber 13 gm, Cholesterol 20 mg, Sodium 1,080 mg

% calories from:

Protein 20%, Carbohydrate 62%, Fat 18% (10 gm fat)

Croque Monsieur
(oven-grilled ham and Swiss)

8 slices French, sourdough, or white bread (whole wheat can also be used)
Prepared mustard to taste (about 2 tsp)
4 oz reduced-fat Swiss cheese or light Jarlsberg
4 oz thinly sliced extra lean ham
No-stick cooking spray (olive oil or butter flavor)

Preheat oven to 450°. Remove crusts from bread if desired. Spread half of bread slices with mustard to taste. Trim cheese slices to fit bread, and place on top of mustard coated slices. Trim ham slices to fit bread; place on cheese. Top with remaining bread slices. Arrange sandwiches on cookie sheet. Spray the top side of sandwich with no-stick cooking spray. Flip over and spray the bottom side of sandwich with cooking spray. Bake for about 5 minutes or until lightly browned. Turn sandwich over and bake a few minutes more. Cut sandwiches into halves and serve warm wrapped individually in small paper napkins. Makes 4 servings.

153

Nutritional analysis per serving:
Calories 284, Fiber 0.7 gm, Cholesterol 29 mg, Sodium 936 mg

% calories from:
Protein 27%, Carbohydrate 51%, Fat 22% (6.8 gm fat). You can lower the fat by 1.5 gm of fat per serving by using light Jarlsberg cheese, or similar, containing 3.5 gm of fat per oz.

Barbecued Pork Sandwiches

These are great noon-time sandwiches for the weekend. During the week they make great dinners. I suggest making a double batch and putting the extra servings in the freezer for a quick dinner.

1 1/4 lb pork tenderloin, cut into 1-inch chunks

1 medium onion, chopped

1 medium green pepper, chopped

1/2 of a 6-oz can tomato paste

1/4 cup packed brown sugar

1 cup nonalcoholic beer

2 Tbsp seasoned rice vinegar (or similar)

1 to 1 1/2 Tbsp chili powder

1/2 tsp salt

1 tsp Worcestershire sauce

1/2 tsp dry mustard

5 6-inch-long rolls (or similar)

Lettuce leaves

In large nonstick saucepan or Dutch oven, combine all ingredients except rolls and lettuce. Bring mixture to boil. Reduce heat immediately to low. Cover and simmer about 2 hours or until pork is very tender, stirring occasionally.

When pork is tender, cool slightly, then shred pork with a spoon, spatula, or your hands. Cut each roll in half. Line the rolls with lettuce. Fill the rolls with the pork mixture. Makes 5 servings.

Nutritional analysis per serving:

Calories 381, Fiber 3 gm, Cholesterol 67 mg, Sodium 752 mg

% calories from:

Protein 31%, Carbohydrate 52%, Fat 15% (6.4 gm fat)

Cold Country Oven Fried Chicken

This chicken smells so good out of the oven it may not make it into the refrigerator for tomorrow's lunch — so you better make 2 batches. If you don't want to use shortening, just take it out completely and generously coat bottom of foil-lined pan with no-stick cooking spray. It will turn out fine without it, but the little amount of shortening seems to add a bit of flavor and keeps the chicken coating from sticking to the foil a bit better.

1/4 cup low-fat milk

1 egg

1 cup flour

1 tsp garlic powder

1 tsp paprika

1/2 tsp poultry seasoning

3/4 tsp black pepper

1 tsp salt

6 chicken breasts, skinless (boneless if desired, but you will have enough egg and flour mixture to coat 8 breasts), if you want to use all or part thighs, remove their skin as well

1 Tbsp butter flavored shortening

No-stick cooking spray

Preheat oven to 325°. Blend milk and egg in medium sized bowl. Combine flour, garlic powder, paprika, poultry seasoning, black pepper, and salt in plastic bag or medium sized bowl. Shake chicken in flour mixture. Dip chicken pieces in milk/egg mixture. Shake chicken a second time in flour mixture to coat well.

Line a 9 x 13" baking pan with foil. Rub 1/2 tablespoon of shortening on the foil, then place chicken on the foil. Generously spray chicken with no-stick cooking spray. Melt the remaining shortening and drizzle evenly over chicken. Bake for about 30 minutes. Turn chicken over and bake an additional 15 to 20 minutes or until chicken is brown on both sides and cooked throughout. Remove from oven and let cool. Wrap well and keep in refrigerator for cold oven fried chicken. Makes 6 servings.

Serving Suggestion:

Serve with a light potato salad or roll, crunchy vegetable sticks, and fresh fruit for a more complete lunch.

Nutritional analysis per serving:

Calories 258, Fiber 0.6 gm, Cholesterol 110 mg, Sodium 352 mg

% calories from:

Protein 49%, Carbohydrate 27%, Fat 24% (6.6 gm fat)

Tuna & Tartar Salad
(for green salad or a sandwich)

Tartar Sauce:
> 1/2 cup light mayonnaise
>
> 1/2 cup low-fat or nonfat mayonnaise
>
> 2 Tbsp minced parsley
>
> 2 Tbsp minced dill pickle (or dill pickle relish)
>
> 2 Tbsp finely minced onion
>
> 1/2 tsp sugar
>
> Pepper to taste
>
> 1Tbsp capers (optional)
>
> 1 Tbsp minced pimento-stuffed olives (optional)

In small bowl, stir above ingredients together until well blended. Makes more than a cup.

158

For Sandwich:

Blend one 6 1/2-ounce can of tuna (packed in water) that has been drained, with 1/4 cup of prepared tartar sauce. Spread half of tuna mixture on a slice of bread. Top with lettuce or tomato then another slice of bread. Repeat to make another sandwich with remaining tuna mixture. Makes 2 sandwiches.

Nutritional analysis per sandwich:

Calories 307, Fiber 6.5 gm, Cholesterol 22.5 mg, Sodium 760 mg

% calories from:

Protein 40%, Carbohydrate 44%, Fat 16% (5.6 gm fat)

For Salad:

Blend one 6 1/2-ounce can of tuna (packed in water) that has been drained, with 1/4 cup of prepared tartar sauce. Place about 2 cups of green salad (make according to your preference) in salad bowl or on dinner plate. Scoop out half of tuna mixture and place in center of salad. Garnish with celery and carrot sticks if desired. Makes two light salads.

Nutritional analysis per salad:

Calories 197, Fiber 4 gm, Cholesterol 22.5 mg, Sodium 414 mg

% calories from:

Protein 63%, Carbohydrate 23%, Fat 14% (3 gm fat)

Spicy Hummus With Crudités and Crackers

1 15 1/2-oz can 50% less-sodium garbanzo beans

3 cloves garlic, minced or pressed

1/3 cup tahini (sesame seed paste)

1/4 cup lemon juice

3 Tbsp light sour cream

2 Tbsp fat-free cream cheese

1/4 tsp seasoning salt (optional)

1/4 tsp ground cumin

1/4 tsp paprika

2 Tbsp finely chopped fresh parsley (optional)

Crudités: choose crisp vegetables like red bell pepper, carrots, celery, cauliflower, broccoli, green beans, etc.

Crackers: choose from the many fat-free and low-fat crackers on the market

Drain garbanzo beans and rinse well (reserve some of the liquid to add back if you need it to make a thinner dip). Place beans, garlic, tahini, lemon juice, sour cream, cream cheese, seasoning salt, cumin, paprika, and parsley in food processor. Process until well blended and somewhat smooth. Add more lemon juice or garbanzo liquid to taste. Use immediately or cover and refrigerate (will keep for several days). Serve with crudités and crackers. Makes about 3 cups of dip.

Nutritional analysis per 1/3 cup serving of dip (not including vegetables/crackers):

Calories 100, Fiber 3 gm, Cholesterol 1 mg, Sodium 118 mg

% calories from:

Protein 3%, Carbohydrate 35%, Fat 51% (5.7 gm fat)

Egg Salad Sandwiches

5 hard cooked eggs (throw away 2 1/2 of the yolks)

2 Tbsp chopped green onion

3 Tbsp low-fat mayonnaise

1 Tbsp Dijon mustard (or similar mustard)

Pepper to taste

2 slices Louis Rich less-fat turkey bacon, cooked till crisp then crumbled (optional)

6 slices whole wheat bread

Lettuce leaves

In small bowl, shred egg whites and 2 1/2 egg yolks into pieces with fork. Add green onion, mayonnaise, mustard, pepper, and bacon. Stir to blend. Spread one-third of egg mixture on a slice of bread. Top with lettuce leaf and another slice of bread. Repeat with remaining egg mixture and bread. Makes 3 sandwiches.

Nutritional analysis per sandwich:

Calories 248, Fiber 4.7 gm, Cholesterol 177 mg, Sodium 663 mg

% calories from:

Protein 23%, Carbohydrate 48%, Fat 29% (7.9 gm fat)

Fast Chili Nachos

1/2 of a 15-oz can fat-free Hormel vegetarian chili

2 oz reduced-fat cheese, grated (sharp cheddar or Monterey Jack)

1 to 2 Tbsp salsa

2 Tbsp light or nonfat sour cream

1 1/2 oz baked tortilla chips

Spread chili in center of a microwave-safe dinner plate. Sprinkle cheese evenly over the chili. Microwave on high for 2 to 3 minutes or until cheese is melted. Spread salsa in center of chili, then place a big dollop of sour cream in center. Spread chips around the chili and serve. Makes 1 serving.

Nutritional analysis per serving:

Calories 537, Fiber 14 gm, Cholesterol 70 mg, Sodium 1,171 mg

% calories from:

Protein 25%, Carbohydrate 51%, Fat 24%, (14.5 gm fat)

Nutritional analysis per serving (using restaurant-style white corn Tostitos instead of baked tortilla chips):

Calories 602, Fiber 14 gm, Cholesterol 70 mg, Sodium 1,275 mg

% calories from:

Protein 25%, Carbohydrate 51%, Fat 31% (21.5 gm fat)

Chicken Nachos

1/2 cup shredded cooked chicken breast (smoked, roasted, stewed, or BBQ chicken)

1/2 cup reduced-fat shredded Monterey Jack cheese

1/8 cup chopped green onions

1 Tbsp fire-roasted canned chopped green chilies, drained

1/4 avocado, cut into chunks (optional)

2 oz low-fat tortilla chips

Chunky salsa

In medium bowl, toss chicken, cheese, green onions, green chilies, and avocado together. Spread tortilla chips evenly over microwave-safe dinner plate. Top with chicken-cheese mixture. Microwave on high about 3 minutes or until cheese is bubbling. Dip chips in salsa as desired. Makes 1 large serving or two snack servings.

Nutritional analysis per serving (including 1/4 cup salsa):

Calories 524, Cholesterol 91 mg, Sodium 788 mg

% calories from:

Protein 33%, Carbohydrate 40%, Fat 27% (15.5 gm fat)

Smoked Chicken (or trout) Salad Sandwich With Dill Dressing

2 to 3 Tbsp light mayonnaise (reduced-fat or fat-free if desired)

2 green onions, finely chopped

1/2 Tbsp fresh dill, finely chopped

1 cup finely shredded smoked chicken breast (or trout)

2 bagels, split and toasted (or two sourdough rolls, or any type bread desired)

Serve with sliced tomatoes and romaine lettuce if desired

Mix mayonnaise, onion, and dill in a small bowl until well blended. Add smoked chicken or trout, and stir gently with fork until blended. Serve with desired bread and garnish. Makes 2 sandwiches.

Nutritional analysis per serving:

Calories 329, Fiber 1.5 gm, Cholesterol 71 mg, Sodium 380 mg

% calories from:

Protein 37%, Carbohydrate 45%, Fat 18% (6.4 gm fat)

Glorified Grilled Cheese

2 slices whole wheat bread or other type bread

1 oz reduced-fat cheese, grated or sliced (with 5 gm fat or less per oz)

1 Tbsp light Alouette garlic & herbs spreadable cheese (or similar)

No-stick cooking spray

Spray one side of bread with no-stick cooking spray. Place bread in thick nonstick frying pan over medium low heat. Place cheese on the bread. While that starts to cook, spread the light Alouette evenly on one side of the remaining slice of bread. Lay on top of the other slice in the pan. Spray top of sandwich with no-stick cooking spray. When bottom is lightly browned, flip the sandwich over. Continue cooking until that side is lightly browned. Makes 1 serving.

NOTE: Fat-free cheese slices also can be used, but most people find the reduced-fat types more acceptable.

Nutritional analysis per sandwich (using cheese with 5 gm of fat per oz):
Calories 275, Fiber 5 gm, Cholesterol 27 mg, Sodium 577 mg

% calories from:
Protein 22%, Carbohydrate 50%, Fat 28% (9 gm fat)

Light Club Sandwich

2 slices Louis Rich less-fat turkey bacon (or similar)

3 slices whole wheat bread

1 Tbsp low-fat mayonnaise (or 1/2 Tbsp light mayonnaise)

2 lettuce leaves

1 large slice turkey breast (no more than 2 oz)

Pepper to taste

1/2 large tomato, sliced

Cook bacon in nonstick frying pan over low heat until crisp. Spread one side of each bread slice with mayonnaise. Arrange lettuce leaf on one slice; top with one slice of turkey; sprinkle with pepper, then cover with another bread slice, mayonnaise side up. Top with another leaf of lettuce, tomato slices, bacon slices, and remaining bread slice, mayonnaise side down. Cut sandwich diagonally into fourths; secure each quarter with decorated toothpicks if desired. Makes 1 sandwich.

Nutritional analysis per sandwich:

Calories 404, Fiber 8 gm, Cholesterol 68 mg, Sodium 1,105 mg

% calories from:

Protein 29%, Carbohydrate 47%, Fat 24% (10.8 gm fat)

Monte Cristo Sandwich

These sandwiches also work well as a brunch item.

1 cup 2% low-fat milk (or similar)

1 egg

1/4 cup fat-free egg substitute

1 tsp Italian herb seasoning (optional)

8 thick slices bread (whole grain, sourdough, or French bread, depending on preference)

1/2 lb sliced turkey breast

4 oz reduced-fat Monterey Jack or Swiss cheese, sliced or grated

No-stick cooking spray

Beat milk, egg, egg substitute and Italian herbs together until smooth. Coat a nonstick frying pan generously with no-stick cooking spray; heat over medium-low heat. Dip bread slices in mixture, then cook until bottom side is golden brown. Flip French toast over to brown other side. Remove slices and cool for a few minutes. Distribute the turkey over 4 slices of French toast. Top each with 1/4 of the cheese. Top with the remaining French toast slices and warm in microwave until cheese melts (about 2 to 3 minutes) or in 325° oven (about 5 to 7 minutes). Makes 4 servings.

Serving Suggestion:

Serve with a fresh fruit salad and vegetable sticks.

Nutritional analysis per serving:

Calories 468, Fiber 1.5 gm, Cholesterol 124 mg, Sodium 761 mg

% calories from:

Protein 33%, Carbohydrate 46%, Fat 21% (10.5 gm fat)

Delightfully Light Dinners

Deluxe (Quick-Fix) Ramen Oriental Soup

1/2 tsp sesame oil

2 cloves garlic, minced or pressed

2/3 cup sliced fresh mushrooms

1/2 cup low-sodium chicken broth

1/8 tsp ground ginger or 1/2 tsp fresh minced ginger

1 cup fresh snow peas (fresh or frozen green beans or
green peas can be substituted)

1/4 cup sliced water chestnuts

2 cups water

1 package Campbell's low-fat Ramen noodle soup,
oriental flavor

1/2 cup cooked shrimp, pork tenderloin, or
very lean ham, finely diced

No-stick cooking spray

Coat a medium sized nonstick saucepan generously with no-stick cooking spray. Heat pan over medium-low heat and pour in sesame oil. Add garlic and mushroom slices. Sauté for a minute, then add chicken broth. Continue to cook, stirring frequently, until mushrooms are tender. Stir in ginger, snow peas, and water chestnuts. Add water, and bring to boil. Add noodles and shrimp, and simmer 4 minutes, stirring occasionally. Remove from heat; stir in half the contents of seasoning packet. Makes 1 large serving (or 2 small servings).

Nutritional analysis per large serving:
Calories 445, Fiber 6 gm, Cholesterol 111 mg, Sodium 929 mg

% calories from:
Protein 20%, Carbohydrate 70%, Fat 10% (5 gm fat)

Deluxe (Quick-Fix) Chicken Noodle Soup

Adding extra chicken and vegetables makes a soup heartier.

- 1 10 3/4-oz can Campbell's Healthy Request chicken noodle soup
- 1 can water
- 1 1/4 cup chopped broccoli
- 1 green onion, chopped
- 1 roasted chicken breast, shredded into bite-sized pieces

Place condensed soup in a medium-sized saucepan. Fill the empty soup can with water, and add to the soup. Stir in broccoli, green onion, and chicken pieces, and bring to boil. Cover and reduce heat to a simmer. Cook 5 minutes or until broccoli is tender. Makes 2 servings.

Serving Suggestion:

To make this more like a meal, serve soup with low-fat wheat crackers or a dinner roll.

Nutritional analysis per serving:

Calories 176, Fiber 3 gm, Cholesterol 55 mg, Sodium 648 mg

% calories from:

Protein 42%, Carbohydrate 30%, Fat 28% (5.5 gm fat)

Nutritional analysis per serving of soup and 8 Stoned Wheat Thin crackers which contain 60 calories and 1.5 gm of fat for every 2 crackers:

Calories 416, Fiber 5 gm, Cholesterol 55 mg, Sodium 928 mg

% calories from:

Protein 24%, Carbohydrate 51%, Fat 25% (11.5 gm fat)

California Roll Sushi

I'm not sure if this type of sushi has caught on in the rest of the country, but it's one of the most popular here in California, thus the name. If you would prefer not to use crabmeat, just substitute strips of cucumber.

1 cup short or medium grain rice, uncooked

1 2/3 cups water

1/2 tsp sesame oil

1/2 tsp salt

2 Tbsp seasoned rice vinegar

1 Tbsp sugar

2 sheets Yaki-Nori (roasted seaweed)

4 thin strips of avocado (about 1/4 avocado)

4 strips of crabmeat or imitation crabmeat, about 1-2 oz (strips of cucumber can be substituted)

Wasabe paste to taste, optional (available in some supermarkets, oriental food stores, specialty stores, and import stores. This green powder comes in a small tin)

Low-sodium soy sauce for dipping (optional)

For Vinegared Rice:

Combine rice, water, sesame oil, and salt in a medium saucepan. Bring to a rolling boil. Reduce heat to low, cover, and simmer 12 to 15 minutes. While rice is cooking, combine vinegar and sugar in a small saucepan, and heat just until sugar is dissolved. When rice is cooked, remove from heat, and stir in vinegar-sugar mixture.

174

To Roll Sushi:

Lay one sheet of roasted seaweed on bamboo roller (you can find these in some supermarkets and also import stores). While rice is still warm, spread half of rice mixture (about 1 1/2 cups) onto seaweed, pressing to flatten, leaving approximately 1 inch of seaweed uncovered on the longest side of the sheet of seaweed. Spread wasabe paste down the center of rice lengthwise if desired. Arrange strips of avocado and crabmeat down the center lengthwise. Start rolling from the side of seaweed that's completely covered with rice, working your way toward the side with plain seaweed at the edge. Make a roll, using the extra seaweed at the edge to wrap around the roll and help seal it. The seaweed should wrap around well since the rice is still warm, but you can coat the plain seaweed with warm water if necessary. Makes 2 rolls. Serve with low-sodium soy sauce and extra wasabe paste if desired.

Nutritional analysis per roll:

Calories 440, Fiber 3.7 gm, Cholesterol 17 mg, Sodium 590 mg

% calories from:

Protein 10%, Carbohydrate 78%, Fat 12% (6 gm fat)

Japanese Chicken Noodle Salad

4 chicken breasts, skinless and boneless

Juice from 1 large or 2 small lemons

1 1/2 Tbsp low-sodium soy sauce

1 cup small macaroni noodles, uncooked

2 portabella mushrooms, or 3 shiitake mushrooms or
1 1/4 cup button mushrooms, sliced

1/2 cup chicken or beef broth, beer, or white wine

1/4 cup chopped green onions

1 1/2 cups chopped celery

1 8-oz can sliced water chestnuts, drained

1/4 tsp seasoned salt

1 1/2 cups snow peas or string beans, with stem removed

1/2 cup low-fat mayonnaise (e.g., Best Foods low-fat with
1 gm fat per Tbsp)

4 Tbsp light mayonnaise

1 Tbsp toasted sesame seeds (toast by heating seeds in
small nonstick pan, stirring constantly, until lightly
browned)

No-stick cooking spray

Cut each chicken breast into about 4 strips. In medium sized bowl, blend lemon juice and soy sauce; add chicken strips. Chill for at least 2 hours, if possible. Broil in foil-lined 9 x 9" baking dish that has been coated with no-stick cooking spray. When top is lightly browned, about 10 minutes, flip chicken strips over and continue to broil until chicken is cooked throughout (about 8 minutes). Let cool, then cut into bit-sized pieces (reserve cooking liquid).

Cook macaroni noodles following package directions; drain. While noodles are boiling, simmer mushrooms in broth, beer, or white wine until tender. In serving bowl, toss chicken and its lemon/soy sauce liquid with macaroni, mushrooms, green onions, celery, water chestnuts, seasoned salt, snow peas, and mayonnaise. Stir to blend well. Sprinkle toasted sesame seeds over the top. Makes 4 servings.

Nutritional analysis per serving:

Calories 370, Fiber 3.3 gm, Cholesterol 78 mg, Sodium 828 mg

% calories from:

Protein 35%, Carbohydrate 39%, Fat 26% (10.7 gm fat)

Superior Meatloaf and Potatoes

1 envelope Lipton onion, beefy onion, or beefy mushroom recipe soup mix

2 lb ground sirloin

4 slices whole wheat bread, finely chopped (1 1/2 cups soft bread crumbs)

1/2 cup fat-free egg substitute

1/2 cup beer

1/2 cup catsup

3-4 cloves garlic, minced or pressed

3/4 tsp black pepper or to taste

1/2 cup tomato sauce or bottled spaghetti sauce with no more than 4 gm fat per 4 oz serving

8 baking potatoes, washed, rubbed very lightly with vegetable oil (about 4 tsp oil will be needed) and wrapped in foil

No-stick cooking spray

NOTE: You can sprinkle dried herbs on potato after rubbing with oil and before wrapping in foil, if desired.

Preheat oven to 350°. In large bowl, combine first eight ingredients (use clean hands if possible to encourage thorough blending). Coat a large shallow baking pan with no-stick cooking spray. Shape beef mixture into a loaf. Bake 1 hour or until cooked throughout. Pour tomato sauce over meat loaf, and bake 5 more minutes. Put potatoes in oven after meat loaf has cooked 15 minutes. Serve meat loaf alongside potato or serve meat loaf on baked potato that has been cut open and spread out slightly onto plate. Makes 8 servings.

Nutritional analysis per serving (including potato):

Calories 502, Fiber 6.3 gm, Cholesterol 76 mg, Sodium 984 mg

% calories from:

Protein 28%, Carbohydrate 54%, Fat 18% (10 gm fat)

One-Pot Mexican Rice & Beans

1 cup chopped onion

1/3 cup chicken or beef broth or beer

1 1/2 cups uncooked rice

1 green pepper, chopped

1 tsp chili powder (increase to 1 1/2 to 2 tsp if you like it spicy)

1/2 cup catsup

1 11-oz can (1 1/2 cups) V-8 picante flavor (or regular V-8 or tomato juice)

2 1/2 cups water

1 Tbsp olive oil

2 cloves garlic, minced or pressed

2 ripe tomatoes, chopped

1 15-oz can pinquitos—small brown beans (1 1/2 cups cooked or canned pinto beans may also be used)

1 cup grated reduced-fat Monterey Jack cheese (sharp cheddar may also be used)

No-stick cooking spray

Coat a large nonstick saucepan with no-stick cooking spray. Add onions and sauté for a minute. Add broth or beer and continue to simmer until onion is golden. Add rice, green pepper, chili powder, catsup, V-8, and water, and bring to a boil. Reduce heat, cover, and simmer 25 minutes or until rice is tender.

Meanwhile, toss olive oil, garlic, tomatoes, beans, and half of cheese together in medium sized bowl. Once rice is tender, stir tomato/bean mixture with rice. Sprinkle remaining cheese over the top. Serves 7.

Nutritional analysis per serving:

Calories 293, Fiber 5 gm, Cholesterol 9 mg, Sodium 708 mg

% calories from:

Protein 14%, Carbohydrate 70%, Fat 16% (5.3 gm fat)

Microwave Zucchini Summer Soup

This soup is nice on a hot summer day for two reasons: it can be made in the microwave and it can even be served chilled.

1 tsp olive oil (optional)

1 cup chopped onion

1 potato, diced

3 cups large diced zucchini

3 cups beef or chicken broth, divided

1 Tbsp lemon juice

1 clove garlic, pressed or minced

Freshly ground pepper to taste

1/2 cup light sour cream

1 tsp dried dillweed, or 2 to 3 tsp fresh dill

Place olive oil if desired along with onion, potato, zucchini, and 1/2 cup of the broth into a 2-3 quart microwave-safe casserole dish or 8-cup glass measure with handle. Cover and microwave on high for 8 minutes or until vegetables are tender. Puree the vegetables along with any liquid in the microwave dish in a food processor or blender. Return to the casserole dish. Add remaining broth, lemon juice, garlic, and pepper. Cover and microwave on high for 6 minutes or until hot. While that's cooking, mix sour cream and dill together in small bowl. Spoon soup into serving dishes and float a couple of spoonfuls of the dill-cream in each bowl. Makes 4 servings.

Serving suggestion:

Serve each serving of soup with a roll to make a complete light dinner.

Nutritional analysis per serving (including roll):

Calories 271, Fiber 4 gm, Cholesterol 5 mg, Sodium 920 mg (to reduce sodium, use low-salt broth)

% calories from:

Protein 16%, Carbohydrate 74%, Fat 10% (3 gm fat)

Nutritional analysis per serving of soup only:

Calories 115, Fiber 3 gm, Cholesterol 4 mg, Sodium 608 mg

% calories from:

Protein 19%, Carbohydrate 69%, Fat 12% (2 gm fat)

10-Minute Ravioli With Marinara

I always have tortellini or small ravioli in my freezer for evenings when I want to throw dinner together in 10 minutes. Just boil your pasta while you microwave or steam some vegetables. Stir in prepared spaghetti or marinara sauce and even some leftover chicken and call it dinner for four!

4 cups cooked tortellini or small ravioli (containing no more than 200 calories and 6 gm of fat per 1-cup serving)

2 cups steamed or microwaved vegetables (zucchini, broccoli, etc.)

2 cups prepared spaghetti marinara or sauce (with no more than 4 gm fat per 1/2 cup or 4 oz serving)

1 cup of leftover chicken (boneless and skinless), shredded into bite-size pieces (optional)

Parmesan cheese (optional)

In medium saucepan place cooked and drained tortellini or ravioli, vegetables, sauce, and chicken. Heat through, while gently stirring. Makes 4 servings. Sprinkle with Parmesan cheese if desired.

184

Nutritional analysis per serving:
Calories 294, Fiber 5 gm, Cholesterol 45 mg, Sodium 730 mg

% calories from:
Protein 13%, Carbohydrate 57%, Fat 30% (10 gm fat)

Quick Tortellini Soup

2 14 1/2-oz cans beef or chicken broth (use a low-sodium version if you prefer)

2 cups water

9 oz (2 1/4 cups) fresh packed or frozen tortellini (containing 6 gm of fat per 3 oz or 3/4 cup serving)

1/2 red pepper, chopped

4 green onions, chopped

2 stalks celery, sliced diagonally

1 large carrot, thinly sliced into coins

3 Tbsp grated Parmesan cheese (optional)

Add all ingredients except cheese to a large saucepan or stockpot. Bring to a boil, then reduce heat to maintain a gentle boil. Cover and cook 15 minutes or until vegetables and tortellini are tender. Spoon into large serving bowls. Sprinkle 1 tablespoon of Parmesan over each serving if desired. Makes 3 large servings.

(185)

Nutritional analysis per serving (using Contadina 3-Cheese Tortellini):

Calories 305, Fiber 3 gm, Cholesterol 35 mg, Sodium 1,240 mg (reduce sodium by using low-salt broth)

% calories from:

Protein 20%, Carbohydrate 60%, Fat 20% (6.8 gm fat)

German Potato Salad

You can make this delightful, low-fat salad more like a light meal just by adding some water-packed tuna.

> 6 medium potatoes (or 8 smaller potatoes)
>
> 5 slices 50% less-fat Louis Rich turkey bacon
>
> 1 cup chopped sweet or yellow onion
>
> 3/4 cup non-alcoholic (or regular) beer, divided
>
> 2 tsp sugar
>
> 1/2 tsp salt
>
> 1 tsp Wondra quick-mixing flour (or regular)
>
> 1/8 tsp pepper
>
> 1/4 cup seasoned rice vinegar (or red wine vinegar)
>
> 1 tsp dried parsley flakes (or 1 Tbsp fresh minced parsley)
>
> 1/2 tsp celery seed
>
> 2 6 1/2-oz cans water-packed tuna (optional)

186

Place potatoes in large saucepan; cover with water. Bring to boiling, then reduce heat to low; cover and simmer 30 minutes or until fork-tender. Drain potatoes, and once cooled, peel and dice potatoes. While potatoes are boiling, cook turkey bacon in a large nonstick frying pan until crisp (using low heat usually produces a crispier, melt-in-your-mouth bacon). Remove bacon from pan and crumble into pieces; set aside.

Add chopped onion to the same frying pan. Cook onion, stirring constantly, until tender (about 5 minutes). Add 1/4 cup of the beer after a couple of minutes. Stir in sugar, salt, flour, and pepper until well blended. Gradually stir in vinegar and 1/2 cup of the beer. Cook, stirring constantly, until it is slightly thickened and boiling. Stir in parsley flakes and celery seed. Gently add in potatoes, bacon, and tuna. Heat through and serve warm. You can also store potato salad in a covered container in refrigerator and serve it chilled. Makes at least 6 servings.

Nutritional analysis per serving:

Calories 194, Fiber 3 gm, Cholesterol 8 mg, Sodium 345 mg

% calories from:

Protein 10%, Carbohydrate 81%, Fat 9% (2 gm fat)

Nutritional analysis per serving (including tuna):

Calories 266, Fiber 3 gm, Cholesterol 18 mg, Sodium 541 mg

% calories from:

Protein 32%, Carbohydrate 60%, Fat 8% fat (2.5 gm fat)

Moist (and Low-fat) Microwave Chicken

For a crispier coating, bake this chicken in a 400-degree oven for 10 minutes.

1/4 cup Hellmann's or Best Foods low-fat mayonnaise
1/4 cup Hellmann's or Best Foods light mayonnaise
2 cloves garlic, minced or crushed
1 Tbsp lemon juice
6 chicken breasts, skinless (and boneless if desired)
1 1/4 cups Italian-seasoned bread crumbs
No-stick cooking spray

Blend two types of mayonnaise, garlic, and lemon juice together in small bowl. Brush chicken on all sides with mayonnaise mixture. Place bread crumbs in large plastic food bag or large bowl. Add chicken 1 piece at a time; shaking well to coat completely. Arrange chicken, the former skin-side up in a 13 x 9" glass baking dish that has been coated with no-stick cooking spray. Coat the top of the chicken with a little no-stick cooking spray. Cover with waxed paper. Microwave on high for 10 minutes. Rotate dish and microwave, uncovered, an additional 10 to 12 minutes or until chicken is tender. Makes 6 servings.

Serving suggestion:

Serve one of the chicken breasts with a green salad and a roll for a more complete meal.

Nutritional analysis per serving:

Calories 247, Fiber 0.5 gm, Cholesterol 76 mg, Sodium 449 mg

% calories from:

Protein 47%, Carbohydrate 25%, Fat 28% (7.6 gm fat)

Artichoke Heart and Bacon Fettuccini

2 tsp butter

3 cloves garlic, minced or pressed

13 3/4-oz can artichoke hearts (drain and pick over the artichoke hearts, discarding the parts that feel tough).

3 Roma tomatoes, diced

1/8 cup milk

3 cups cooked fettuccini noodles (or similar)

1/4 cup grated Parmesan cheese

3 or 4 strips Louis Rich less-fat turkey bacon, cooked crisp then crumbled

Melt butter in large nonstick saucepan. Add garlic, artichoke hearts, and tomatoes; cook over medium-low heat, stirring often for about 4 minutes. Pour the milk into the artichoke heart mixture and stir to blend. Stir in cooked noodles, Parmesan cheese, and crumbled bacon. Makes 3 servings.

189

Nutritional analysis per serving:

Calories 310, Fiber 8.7 gm, Cholesterol 15 mg, Sodium 423 mg

% calories from:

Protein 18%, Carbohydrate 59%, Fat 25% (9.5 gm fat)

Pork Tenderloin Florentine

1 1/4 lb pork tenderloin (about 1 1/2 whole tenderloins)
Flour
1 Tbsp olive oil
1 cup chicken broth
4 Tbsp Wondra flour (quick-mixing flour)
1/2 tsp pepper
Approx. 1 1/4 cups whole milk
1 10-oz box frozen chopped spinach
1 egg yolk
1/4 cup fat-free egg substitute
1 cup grated reduced-fat Swiss cheese (4 oz)
About 3 cups cooked rice or noodles
Olive oil no-stick cooking spray

Cut each tenderloin in half lengthwise, then in half width-wise to make 4 pork chop-shaped servings of meat. You should have approximately 6 servings of pork. Dredge chops in flour. In a large nonstick frying pan with cover or Dutch oven, heat olive oil over medium-high heat; spread around bottom of pan with spatula. Add tenderloin pork chops. Spray chops with no-stick cooking spray. Cook until bottom is well browned. Flip chops over and brown other side. (If the pork chops need moisture, add a couple tablespoons of the chicken broth.) Add all of chicken broth and reduce heat; cover pan and simmer 30 minutes, turning chops every 10 or so minutes.

190

Remove pork chops with fork and set aside. Measure the remaining broth from pan in a 2-cup measure. Add enough milk to total 2 cups (broth plus milk together should measure 2 cups); add to medium nonstick saucepan. Stir in the flour and pepper. Heat to boiling over medium heat, stirring constantly. Boil and stir 1 minute to thicken.

Preheat oven to 350°. Microwave spinach in box or microwave-safe container until hot (about 5 minutes). Drain well. Coat 9 x 9" baking dish with no-stick cooking spray. Spread spinach on the bottom of pan. Place chops evenly on top. Beat egg yolk with egg substitute and stir into white sauce; pour over chops. Sprinkle with Swiss cheese. Bake in oven until sauce bubbles (about 15 minutes). Serve each portion over 1/2 cup of cooked rice or noodles. Makes 6 servings.

Nutritional analysis per serving (including rice):
Calories 422, Fiber 2 gm, Cholesterol 107 mg, Sodium 305 mg

% calories from:
Protein 34%, Carbohydrates 40%, Fat 26% (12 gm fat)

Seafood Risotto

3-4 cloves garlic, minced or pressed

1/2 cup white wine

1 bottle (8 oz) clam juice

1/4 tsp ground pepper

1/3 lb sea scallops, halved and cut horizontally if large scallops

1/2 lb shrimp or prawns, cooked (if buying the shrimp raw, make sure it is shelled and deveined, and cook it with the scallops in the recipe)

2 1/4 cups water

1 Tbsp butter or margarine

1 leek, chopped

1 cup arborio rice (short grain), dry

Two pinches saffron

2 Tbsp chopped fresh parsley, finely chopped

1/4 cup grated Parmesan cheese

No-stick cooking spray

Coat medium-sized nonstick saucepan with no-stick cooking spray. Heat over medium-low heat. Add garlic and simmer about a minute; be careful not to brown garlic. Add wine and bring to boil. Add the clam juice and pepper and return to boil. Stir in scallops (and shrimp if uncooked) and cook, stirring constantly, for about 3 minutes or until scallops are just cooked throughout. Add shrimp, and toss to mix. Transfer seafood mixture to a bowl with a slotted spoon and set aside. Add water to the saucepan, and bring to simmer (keep temperature on low to maintain the simmer).

In separate medium-sized nonstick saucepan, melt the butter. Add the leek and sauté for a few minutes. Stir in the dry rice and sauté, stirring constantly, for a couple of minutes. Add 1/2 cup of the simmering liquid and continue cooking until the liquid is almost absorbed. Continue adding the liquid, 1/2 cup at a time, until all the liquid is gone and the rice is completely cooked. Add the saffron to the last 1/2-cup measure of the clam juice mixture before mixing it into the rice mixture. Total cooking time should be about 16 to 20 minutes. If the rice is not fully cooked, add 1/4 cup of hot water and stir until absorbed. Stir in shrimp and scallop mixture and parsley. Sprinkle Parmesan cheese over the rice; cover, and let sit off the heat for about 10 minutes (to help blend flavors). Makes 4 servings.

Nutritional analysis per serving:
Calories 346, Fiber 1.2 gm, Cholesterol 136 mg, Sodium 617 mg

% calories from:
Protein 29%, Carbohydrate 48%, Fat 16% (6 gm fat)

Cabbage Rolls

1 large cabbage or 2 small cabbages

1 lb ground sirloin

2 cups cooked white rice

5 green onions, chopped

4 cloves garlic, minced or pressed

Pepper to taste

1/3 cup low-sodium chicken broth, divided

1 15-oz can tomato sauce

1 6-oz can Italian-style (or regular) tomato paste

1 28-oz can whole tomatoes, break tomatoes in half with
    spoon

1/3 cup brown sugar, packed

Juice from 1 lemon

Preheat oven to 325°. Core cabbage and add to large pot
filled halfway with water. Bring to boil and cover pot. Boil
about 20 minutes or until leaves are softened. Drain on
towels. While cabbage is boiling, blend beef, cooked rice,
green onions, garlic, pepper, and 1/4 cup of chicken broth
together well (use hands if possible).

Place remaining chicken broth, tomato sauce, tomato
paste, tomatoes (including liquid), brown sugar, and
lemon juice in medium sized roasting pan. Stir well to
blend.

Separate 30 to 32 leaves from cabbage. Lay out one of the
leaves on a cutting board. Take a rounded tablespoon of
beef mixture and place in center of leaf. Tuck side of the
leaf in and roll the leaf starting with the thicker part and

194

ending with the thinner top of the leaf. Place seam side
down in roasting pan. Repeat with remaining cabbage
leaves and beef mixture (using a level tablespoon of beef
mixture for the smaller leaves). Spoon tomato mixture
over cabbage rolls and cover roasting pan. Bake for about
1 1/2 to 2 hours, or until beef is completely cooked. Makes
about 32 rolls (8 servings).

Nutritional analysis per serving:

Calories 268, Fiber 6 gm, Cholesterol 38 mg, Sodium 583 mg

% calories from:

Protein 26%, Carbohydrate 60%, Fat 14% (4.5 gm fat)

Chicken Cream Cheese Rolls

This recipe is so simple yet so delicious. Best of all—it makes its own savory sauce that can be drizzled on top before serving.

4 chicken breasts, boned and skinned

1 small onion, peeled and cut into about 10 slices

4 oz light or fat-free cream cheese

1 Tbsp fresh chives, finely chopped

1 1/2 tsp fresh basil, finely chopped (if using bottled basil, use 1 tsp)

4 slices Louis Rich less-fat turkey bacon (or similar)

No-stick cooking spray

Preheat oven to 400°. Line a 9 x 9 x 2" baking pan with foil. Coat the foil generously with no-stick cooking spray. Place chicken between waxed paper and pound to no thicker than 1/2" (or have your butcher do it for you). Set aside.

Coat a sheet of foil (about 9 x 13") generously with no-stick cooking spray. Lay onion slices evenly over foil. Spray with no-stick cooking spray. Broil until top is light brown, watching carefully. Flip slices over and let second side brown. Remove from heat. Let cool.

Blend onions, cream cheese, chives, and basil in a small food processor until smooth. If you don't have a small food processor, finely chop the onion slices and blend all the ingredients together well with mixer.

Spread about 1/8 cup of the onion mixture over each chicken breast. Gently roll up each breast (being careful not to roll it up so tightly that the onion mixture squeezes out). Wrap 1 slice of bacon around each breast roll. Place chicken seam side down in prepared pan. Bake in top portion of oven for about 40 minutes or until chicken is cooked throughout. Broil a couple of minutes to brown bacon if needed. Makes 4 servings. Serve with steamed rice or cooked noodles.

Nutritional analysis per serving using light cream cheese (not including rice or noodles):

Calories 253, Fiber 0.5 gm, Cholesterol 98 mg, Sodium 405 mg

% calories from:

Protein 53%, Carbohydrate 10%, Fat 37% (10.5 gm fat)

Easy Ham & Potato Casserole

This recipe is a great way to use up leftover ham. I always have the rest of the ingredients on hand.

6 Tbsp light or fat-free sour cream
2 eggs
1/4 cup fat-free egg substitute
3 Tbsp flour
1/2 tsp pepper
1/2 tsp salt (optional)
1 cup low-fat milk
1 1/2 cups diced lean ham, trimmed of visible fat
8 spring onions, chopped
4 cups shredded, peeled potatoes or use Ore-Ida country style hash browns, thawed
1/2 cup reduced-fat sharp cheddar cheese or other reduced-fat cheese
No-stick cooking spray

198

Preheat oven to 350°. Generously coat a 9 x 9 x 2" baking pan with no-stick cooking spray. Blend sour cream, eggs, egg substitute, flour, and pepper in mixing bowl on medium speed until smooth. Slowly add in milk, and blend until smooth. Stir in remaining ingredients (ham, onions, potatoes, and cheese). Spoon into prepared pan, spreading the potato mixture evenly in pan. Bake for 50 to 60 minutes or until nicely browned. Makes 4 large servings.

Nutritional analysis per serving:
Calories 354, Fiber 3 gm, Cholesterol 140 mg, Sodium 792 mg

% calories from:
Protein 27%, Carbohydrate 50%, Fat 23% (9 gm fat)

Spicy Salmon Steaks

This salmon tastes great hot or at room temperature.

3 Tbsp Dijon-style mustard (regular prepared mustard can be substituted)

3 Tbsp low-sodium soy sauce

4 Tbsp dark brown sugar, packed

3 Tbsp Madeira wine (dry white wine or nonalcoholic beer or wine can be substituted)

4 salmon steaks (about 6-8 oz each)

No-stick cooking spray

In medium sized flat bottomed dish or bowl, mix mustard, soy sauce, brown sugar, and wine together until well blended. Add salmon steaks and cover with plastic wrap or foil. Marinate fish in refrigerator up to 6 hours. If broiling salmon, line your broiling dish with foil. Coat the foil with no-stick cooking spray. Place salmon on foil and broil about 5 minutes on first side. Turn and brush with remaining marinade. Broil second side until fish flakes easily (about 8 minutes more, depending on size of steaks). Serve with steamed rice and vegetables or a salad to complete your dinner. Makes 4 servings.

199

Nutritional analysis per serving (if steaks are 6 oz each):
Calories 307, Fiber 0, Cholesterol 62 mg, Sodium 612 mg

% calories from:
Protein 49%, Carbohydrate 20%, Fat 31% (10 gm fat)

Four-Can Beef & Bean Enchiladas

Usually the idea of using canned food in a recipe isn't exactly something you want broadcasted in a recipe title. But this recipe is so quick and so delicious, I just had to include it in the title to show how convenient it is!

1 onion, chopped

1 lb ground sirloin

2 tsp minced or pressed garlic

1 15-oz can pinquitos, pinto beans, or similar

1 15-oz can Mexican-style stewed tomatoes, undrained

1 4-oz can diced green chilies (mild, medium or hot, according to preference)

1 10-oz can enchilada sauce

12 corn tortillas

2 cups grated reduced-fat sharp cheddar and reduced-fat Monterey Jack cheese, mixed (or use one or the other)

No-stick cooking spray

Preheat oven to 350°. Coat a 13 x 9" baking pan with no-stick cooking spray; set aside. Spray large high quality nonstick saucepan generously with no-stick cooking spray. Add onion and beef, and cook over medium heat, stirring and crumbling beef often. Once beef has browned, add garlic, beans, tomatoes, chilies, and enchilada sauce. Cook and stir until sauce is heated through (about 3 minutes).

Arrange 4 tortillas to cover the bottom of the prepared pan (they will overlap some). Cover with 1/3 of meat mixture. Repeat layers of corn tortillas and beef mixture two more times. Top with grated cheese. Cover pan with foil and bake for 30 to 35 minutes. Makes 8 servings.

Nutritional analysis per serving:

Calories 375, Fiber 11 gm, Cholesterol 53 mg, Sodium 522 mg

% calories from:

Protein 30%, Carbohydrate 45%, Fat 25% (10.9 gm fat)

BBQ Chicken in Winter (using the oven)

*When the chicken and sauce go in the oven it is hard to believe it
will turn out just like BBQ chicken—but it does! The chicken is
nicely glazed with sauce, just as if it was grilled on a barbecue.*

6 chicken breasts, skinless and boneless

Salt and pepper to taste

1 Tbsp butter or margarine

1 Tbsp Worcestershire sauce

1 Tbsp lemon juice

4 Tbsp water

2 Tbsp molasses

1 Tbsp brown sugar

2 Tbsp vinegar

1/4 cup catsup

1/2 Tbsp mustard

No-stick cooking spray

202

Preheat oven to 350°. Coat a 13 x 9" baking pan generously with no-stick cooking spray. Spread the chicken
breasts out in the prepared pan. Season with salt and pepper as desired.

Place remaining ingredients in medium sized nonstick
saucepan (butter, Worcestershire sauce, lemon juice,
water, molasses, brown sugar, vinegar, catsup, and mustard) and bring to boil. Remove from heat. Pour sauce
over chicken pieces, and bake uncovered for 45 minutes
to an hour or until chicken is nicely glazed and cooked

throughout. Turn chicken after 30 minutes of baking. Makes 6 servings.

Nutritional analysis per serving:

Calories 194, Fiber 0.2 gm, Cholesterol 78 mg, Sodium 222 mg

% calories from:

Protein 57%, Carbohydrate 19%, Fat 24% (5 gm fat)

Sweet and Sour Pork With Rice

2 pork tenderloins (about 1 1/4 lb altogether) cut into large bite-sized pieces

6 Tbsp cornstarch

1 Tbsp canola oil

No-stick cooking spray

Meat Marinade:

1 egg yolk

1 Tbsp cornstarch

1 Tbsp low-sodium soy sauce

1 Tbsp honey

1 tsp minced or crushed garlic

Dash of pepper

Sweet and Sour Sauce:

8 Tbsp sugar

1 1/2 Tbsp cornstarch

3/4 tsp salt

3 Tbsp vinegar

3 Tbsp low-sodium soy sauce

3 Tbsp catsup

3/4 cup water or unsweetened pineapple juice

1 green pepper, cut into large bite-sized chunks

5 slices canned pineapple, drained (reserve juice to use in place of water if desired)

At least 5 cups cooked rice

For marinade, combine egg yolk, 1 tablespoon cornstarch, soy sauce, honey, garlic, and pepper in medium sized bowl. Add pork tenderloin pieces, and marinate in refrigerator for at least an hour. Place 6 tablespoons cornstarch in small bowl. Dip each pork cube in cornstarch, and place on paper towel lined plate until all of pork is covered with cornstarch.

Spray bottom of large nonstick frying pan generously with no-stick cooking spray. Add canola oil to the pan, and heat on medium heat. Spread oil with spatula to cover the bottom. When oil is hot, add pork pieces, spreading them in single layer. Once bottom side of pork is brown, flip pork over to brown the other side. Once pork is cooked throughout, turn off heat.

Sweet and sour sauce:
In medium saucepan, combine sugar, cornstarch, and salt; stir. Add vinegar, soy sauce, catsup, and water or pineapple juice, and stir. Bring to a boil. Cook until thickened, stirring frequently. Stir in green pepper, pineapple pieces, and pork, and heat through over low heat. Serve over cooked rice. Makes 5 servings.

Nutritional analysis per serving:
Calories 620, Fiber 2 gm, Cholesterol 106 mg, Sodium about 900 mg

% calories from:
Protein 20%, Carbohydrate 68%, Fat 12% (8 gm fat)

Quick Crab Crepes

1/2 cup low-fat milk, divided

4 tsp Wondra quick-mixing flour

Pinch of seasoning salt

1/8 tsp garlic powder

Pinch or two of black pepper

1 6-oz can crabmeat, drained

2 green onions, chopped

2 Tbsp grated Parmesan cheese

1/4 cup grated part-skim Jarlsberg cheese (optional)

6 No-Cholesterol Crepes (recipe follows)

Blend 1/4 cup of milk with flour in small microwave-safe bowl, and stir until smooth. Add remaining milk and seasoning salt, garlic powder, and pepper. Microwave on high for 1 minute. Stir and microwave 1 minute longer or until thickened. Stir in crabmeat, onions, Parmesan cheese, and Jarlsberg cheese if desired. Spoon some of the crab mixture down the center of each crepe, and roll up. Microwave each serving of crab crepes to heat throughout. Makes about 6 crepes (about 2 servings).

Nutritional analysis per serving (3 crepes):

Calories 273, Cholesterol 68 mg, Sodium 485 mg

% calories from:

Protein 37%, Carbohydrate 40%, Fat 23% (6.9 gm fat)

No-Cholesterol Crepes:

2 egg whites

1 cup flour

Pinch of salt

1/4 cup fat-free egg substitute

1 1/4 cups low-fat milk, divided

No-stick cooking spray

Beat egg whites until stiff; set aside. Combine flour and salt. In mixing bowl, beat egg substitute with 1/2 cup of milk. Add flour and salt mixture to egg mixture, and beat until smooth. Add remaining milk, and beat thoroughly to incorporate air into mixture. Beat in the egg whites on low speed just until blended with batter. Let batter sit out 30 minutes or so if possible.

Coat a small nonstick frying pan generously with no-stick cooking spray. Heat pan until a drop of water dances on the surface. Pour about 1/8 cup of batter into center of pan (the batter should cover the bottom when the pan is tilted). When the batter is no longer runny, loosen the edge and flip the crepe over. Cook the second side about 20 seconds longer. Makes about 18 crepes.

207

Nutritional analysis per crepe:

Calories 38, Fiber 0.2 gm, Cholesterol 1 mg, Sodium 21 mg

% calories from:

Protein 44%, Carbohydrate 33%, Fat 23% (0.4 gm fat)

Sun-Dried Tomato Pesto

This pesto makes a quick, one-dish dinner. Just toss the pesto with hot noodles and steamed vegetables!

1/2 cup julienne strips sun-dried tomatoes (bought dried in a bag)

1/2 cup water

2-3 cloves garlic (1 tsp minced or crushed)

1 cup basil leaves, rinsed and packed

1/4 cup Italian parsley leaves, rinsed and packed

4 tsp olive oil

1/8 to 1/4 cup toasted pine nuts (optional)

1/3 cup Parmesan cheese, shredded or grated

Low-fat milk or low-calorie Italian dressing (optional)

Place dried tomatoes and water in small, microwave-safe bowl. Microwave on high for 1 minute. Let sit 10 minutes. Place tomatoes and liquid in food processor or blender. Add garlic, basil, parsley, olive oil, pine nuts (if desired), and Parmesan cheese. Pulse just until blended. Add low-fat milk or low-calorie Italian dressing if more moisture is needed. Makes 4 servings of pesto to be served with hot noodles, tortellini, fish, as a dressing for sandwiches, etc.

Nutritional analysis per serving of pesto:

Calories 102, Fiber 2 gm, Cholesterol 6.5 mg, Sodium 361 mg

% calories from:

Protein 21%, Carbohydrate 25%, Fat 54% (6 gm fat)

Herb-Roasted Pork Tenderloin

1 large pork tenderloin (about 1 1/4 lb)
1 Tbsp diet margarine
2 Tbsp fresh sage, minced
2 Tbsp fresh thyme leaves, minced
1 tsp garlic, minced
1 Tbsp honey
Salt and pepper to taste
1/2 lemon
No-stick cooking spray

Preheat oven to 275°. Line a loaf pan with foil and spray foil with no-stick cooking spray. Lay tenderloin in loaf pan. In custard cup or small bowl, blend margarine, sage, thyme, garlic, honey, salt, and pepper. Spread half of mixture over top of tenderloin. Flip tenderloin over and spread remaining herb mixture on other side. Squeeze lemon over length of tenderloin. Bake 45 minutes, uncovered. Increase temperature to 425° for 20 more minutes or until browned. Let rest 5 minutes, then cut into slices. Makes 4 servings.

NOTE: Make 2 tenderloins at one time and you'll have some leftover for sandwiches the next day.

Nutritional analysis per serving:
Calories 202, Cholesterol 83 mg, Sodium 119 mg

% calories from:
Protein 60%, Carbohydrate 9%, Fat 31% (7 gm fat)

Herb-Roasted Potatoes

12 small red potatoes (approximately 1 1/4 lb), halved or
    quartered

2 tsp fresh sage leaves, finely chopped

2 tsp fresh thyme leaves, finely chopped

1/2 tsp minced or crushed garlic

1 tsp non-alcoholic beer (or chicken or beef broth or
    wine)

Olive oil no-stick cooking spray (or other similar cooking
    spray)

Preheat oven to 275°. Line a 9 x 9" baking dish or a cake
pan with foil. Coat the foil generously with no-stick cooking spray. Place potatoes in medium sized bowl. Spray the
potatoes generously with no-stick cooking spray. Toss
potatoes in bowl and spray again with no-stick cooking
spray. In small bowl, stir sage, thyme, garlic, and beer
together. Add to bowl with potatoes, and toss well to coat
potatoes with herb mixture. Spoon potatoes into prepared
pan, cut-side down when possible. Bake for about 45 minutes. Increase temperature to 425°, and bake 20 minutes
more or until potatoes are tender and bottom of potatoes
are nicely browned. Makes 4 servings.

Nutritional analysis per serving:

Calories 185, Fiber 4 gm, Cholesterol 0, Sodium 15 mg

% calories from:

Protein 8%, Carbohydrate 91%, Fat 1% (0.2 gm fat)

Hot Dogs in a Biscuit Blanket

2 cups reduced-fat Bisquick

3/4 cup low-fat buttermilk (regular low-fat milk can also
be used)

6-8 turkey hot dogs, 50% less fat (Louis Rich turkey
franks)

No-stick cooking spray

Preheat oven to 375°. Blend Bisquick with buttermilk.
Knead on floured cutting board until smooth. Roll or
press dough out to a rectangle about 1/4" thick and about
5 or 6" long (the length of the hot dog). Cut the dough off
about 3 1/2" from the end (to make a rectangle 5 to 6" x 3
1/2"). Roll one end of dough around a hot dog, and when
the ends meet, press together to seal side and ends of hot
dog. Repeat until all hot dogs are wrapped in biscuit
dough. Place on baking sheet that has been coated with
no-stick cooking spray. Bake about 15 minutes or until
biscuit wrapping is lightly browned. Makes at least 6 servings. Serve with catsup, mustard, and other low-fat dipping sauces.

Nutritional analysis per serving (when 6 per recipe):
Calories 272, Fiber <1 gm, Cholesterol 51 mg, Sodium 1,122 mg

% calories from:
Protein 17%, Carbohydrate 48%, Fat 35% (10.5 gm fat)

Chicken Curry Biscuit Pie

Biscuit Crust:

2 cups reduced-fat Bisquick

3/4 cup low-fat buttermilk (regular low-fat milk can also be used)

Chicken Filling:

2 tsp olive oil

3 cups sliced crimini or shiitake mushrooms, sliced (button mushrooms can also be used)

1 bottle nonalcoholic beer, divided (chicken broth can be substituted)

2 tsp curry powder

2 carrots, diced

2/3 cup fresh or frozen corn

1 cup fresh or frozen sweet peas

1 1/2 cups finely diced potatoes

3 chicken breasts, skinless and boneless, cooked and diced (breasts can be poached in chicken broth or water with a few tablespoons of lemon juice added)

Salt and pepper to taste

2 Tbsp Wondra flour (quick-mixing flour)

2/3 cup whole milk (low-fat milk can be substituted)

1 Tbsp minced parsley (1 tsp dried)

Olive oil no-stick cooking spray

Preheat oven to 375°. Mix Bisquick with buttermilk. Knead a few times on cutting board dusted with flour. Roll dough out to about a 1/4" thickness. Invert a 9" cake pan over dough and use a knife to trace the top of the pan. Set 9" circle of dough aside (this will be the top crust).

Coat cake pan with no-stick cooking spray. Press remaining dough in bottom of pan.

Heat olive oil in large nonstick pan. Add mushroom slices. Sauté for a couple minutes. Add 1/2 cup nonalcoholic beer, and simmer mushrooms until almost tender. Add more beer for moisture if needed. Add curry powder, vegetables, and chicken, and stir to mix. Season with salt and pepper to taste. Add remaining beer and continue to simmer mixture over medium heat for 3 to 5 minutes. Remove from heat.

Spoon out 1/3 cup of beer broth from the vegetables into a glass measuring cup or small bowl. Stir in flour. Stir in milk. Microwave on high for 2 minutes. Stir, then microwave another 2 minutes or until thickened. Stir in parsley. Pour gravy over chicken and vegetable mixture, and stir to mix.

Pour mixture into prepared pan with bottom crust. Place reserved top crust over chicken-vegetable mixture. Cut a few steam vent holes in dough. Bake for 15 to 20 minutes or until golden brown. Makes 6 servings.

213

Nutritional analysis per serving:
Calories 363, Fiber 4.5 gm, Cholesterol 41 mg, Sodium 581 mg

% calories from:
Protein 25%, Carbohydrate 57%, Fat 18% (7 gm fat)

Indonesian Style Chicken & Pork With Peanut Sauce

1/2 cup reduced-fat creamy peanut butter (Jif)

1/2 cup low-sodium soy sauce

1 tsp minced ginger

1 tsp minced or pressed garlic

3 Tbsp honey

1/8 tsp red pepper flakes, or to taste (optional)

10 chicken breasts, boneless and skinless, or 5 chicken breasts and 1 1/2 lb lean center cut pork chops (country-style ribs also work great)

Combine peanut butter, soy sauce, ginger, garlic, honey, and red pepper flakes, if desired, in small nonstick saucepan. Over medium-low heat, cook, stirring constantly, until blended and smooth. Remove from heat. Coat chicken and/or pork with about half of the peanut marinade. Pour the remaining half of the peanut mixture into a serving bowl and set aside until meat is being served (use it for garnishing or dipping). Let meat marinade in peanut mixture in refrigerator until ready to cook. Barbecue, grill, or broil meat until cooked throughout. Makes 10 small servings or 5 large servings. Serve with steamed rice and grilled vegetables for a light dinner.

Nutritional analysis per small serving (using chicken breast only):

Calories 236, Fiber 0.8 gm, Cholesterol 73 mg, Sodium 596 mg

% calories from:

Protein 51%, Carbohydrate 19%, Fat 30% (7.8 gm fat)

Nutritional analysis per small serving (using chicken and lean pork loin chops):

Calories 290, Fiber 0.8 gm, Cholesterol 84 mg, Sodium 598 mg

% calories from:

Protein 44%, Carbohydrate 16%, Fat 40% (12.8 gm fat)

"No More Boil" Vegetable Lasagna

3 cups low-fat bottled spaghetti sauce (with 4 gm fat or less per 4 oz serving)

1/2 cup nonalcoholic beer, regular beer, or white wine

1 onion, chopped

1 pound zucchini, sliced

4 cups fresh mushrooms, sliced

1 15-oz container low-fat ricotta cheese

1 cup (4 oz) grated low-fat mozzarella cheese, divided

1/3 cup grated Parmesan cheese, divided

1/4 cup chopped fresh parsley or 2 Tbsp dry parsley

1/2 cup fresh basil leaves, chopped (optional)

1/4 cup fat-free egg substitute

1/2 tsp salt (optional)

1/4 tsp pepper

9 to 10 (8 oz) Mueller's or Napolina lasagna noodles, uncooked

216

Preheat oven to 350°. In large saucepan combine spaghetti sauce, beer, onion, zucchini, and mushrooms. Bring to boil over medium heat, stirring occasionally. Reduce heat, cover, and simmer 10 minutes.

In medium sized bowl, combine ricotta, 3/4 cup mozzarella, 2 Tbsp Parmesan, parsley, basil, egg, salt, and pepper.

In 13 x 9" baking dish, layer 1 cup vegetable sauce, 3 strips of uncooked noodles, and half of the cheese mixture. Repeat layers once except add 1 1/2 cup sauce. Top with remaining noodles, vegetable sauce, mozzarella, and

Parmesan. Cover tightly and bake for 35 minutes. Uncover and bake 15 minutes longer. Let stand 10 minutes. Makes 8 servings.

Nutritional analysis per serving:

Calories 283, Fiber 3 gm, Cholesterol 21 mg, Sodium 399 mg

% calories from:

Protein 26%, Carbohydrate 49%, Fat 25% (7.9 gm fat)

Grilled Fish with Light Mustard Sauce

1 1/2 to 2 lb fish steaks, about 1" thick

1/4 cup whole milk

1 Tbsp Dijon mustard

1Tbsp Cremora Lite non-dairy creamer

1/4 cup dry white wine

1/2 Tbsp butter or margarine

Salt and pepper to taste

Olive oil no-stick cooking spray

Line a 9 x 9" baking pan or pie pan with foil. Spray foil with no-stick cooking spray. Pat fish with towels, then lay fish in prepared pan. Spray with no-stick spray. Broil fish about 4 to 6 inches from heat, turning once, about 8 minutes each side. Fish should flake readily when poked with a fork in its thickest part.

While fish is broiling, blend milk, mustard, and creamer in a medium nonstick saucepan. Heat over medium heat. Stir in wine (mixture will seem curdled, but it will boil together into a smooth sauce). Boil rapidly, uncovered, until reduced by half. Remove from heat. Stir in butter. Season with salt and pepper. Spoon over fish. Makes about 4 servings.

Serving suggestion:

Serve with low-fat tartar sauce (page 151) instead of light mustard sauce, if desired.

Nutritional analysis per serving (using halibut):

Calories 228, Cholesterol 60 mg, Sodium 163 mg

% calories from:

Protein 70%, Carbohydrate 6%, Fat 24% (6 gm fat)

Dinner Pancakes

2 eggs, separated
2 cups flour (use half white and half whole wheat if desired)
1 tsp salt
1/4 cup fat-free egg substitute
1 1/2 cups low-fat milk
1/4 cup maple syrup (pancake syrup can also be used)
2 cups finely chopped zucchini
1 cup finely chopped onion

In mixing bowl, beat egg whites until glossy peaks form. Spoon from mixing bowl into another bowl and set aside. In separate bowl, blend flour and salt together. Add egg yolks, egg substitute, milk, and maple syrup to mixing bowl (you don't have to clean away any remaining egg white), and beat until blended. Add the dry ingredients and beat vigorously until it's light and fluffy. Stir in the vegetables then fold in the whipped egg whites.

Coat a nonstick frying pan generously with no-stick cooking spray (or lightly grease with butter or margarine). Heat over medium-low heat. When hot, pour about 1/3 cup of batter into pan to make a large pancake. Repeat until pan is filled or batter is gone. Makes 10 very large pancakes (5 servings).

NOTE: Another tasty combination is 2 cups finely chopped broccoli florets and 1 cup finely chopped red bell pepper.

Nutritional analysis per serving (for either vegetable combination):
Calories 315, Fiber 2.5 gm, Cholesterol 90 mg, Sodium 517 mg

% calories from:
Protein 16%, Carbohydrate 72%, Fat 12% (4 gm fat)

Meat & Potato Casserole

1 lb ground sirloin

1 large onion, chopped

4 oz part-skim Jarlsberg cheese (or reduced-fat cheddar cheese)

1/3 cup Parmesan cheese

3 tsp minced or pressed garlic (6 to 8 cloves garlic)

1 Tbsp thyme leaves

3 bay leaves, crushed

1/4 cup low-fat mayonnaise

1/4 cup water

3-4 lb white thin-skinned potatoes, thinly sliced

Black pepper to taste

2 low-sodium beef bouillon packets (2 tsp powder) or cubes dissolved in 1 cup of hot water

No-stick cooking spray

Preheat oven to 375°. Coat a 9 x 13" baking pan with no-stick cooking spray. Set aside. Coat a large frying pan with no-stick cooking spray. Add beef, crumbled, and onion; cook, stirring often until cooked throughout. Set aside. Grind Jarlsberg and Parmesan cheeses together in a food processor, and set aside (or grate the Jarlsberg cheese and mix with Parmesan). Blend garlic, thyme, bay leaves, mayonnaise, and water in small bowl and set aside.

Layer one half of potatoes in bottom of prepared baking pan. Top with half of the cheese. Sprinkle pepper to taste over the cheese. Spread half of the beef mixture evenly over the cheese. Drizzle half of the herb-mayonnaise mixture over the top. Repeat the layers of potatoes, cheese, pepper, beef, and herb-mayonnaise with remaining ingredients. Pour beef broth evenly over the top of the casserole. Cover tightly with foil and bake 60 minutes or until potatoes are tender. Makes 8 servings.

Nutritional analysis per serving:

Calories 378, Fiber 5 gm, Cholesterol 52 mg, Sodium 210 mg

% calories from:

Protein 24%, Carbohydrate 56%, Fat 20% (8 gm fat)

Quick Less-Fat Vegetable Matzo Ball Soup

1 egg

1/4 cup fat-free egg substitute

1 Tbsp oil

1 Tbsp chicken broth

1 packet matzo ball mix (each packet makes about 12 matzo balls)

8 cups less-sodium chicken broth (e.g., Natural Goodness 100% fat-free canned chicken broth)

3 carrots, sliced

3 stalks celery, sliced

1 large onion, chopped

1 cup leftover vegetables (1 chopped tomato and 1/2 cup snow peas)

1/3 cup rice

In small bowl, blend egg, egg substitute, oil, and 1 table-spoon chicken broth with a fork. Add contents of one matzo ball packet, and stir with fork until evenly mixed. Place bowl in refrigerator for 15 minutes.

While matzo ball mixture is chilling, bring 8 cups chicken broth and all the remaining ingredients to a boil.

Once matzo ball mixture is ready, wet hands and form batter into balls approximately 1" in diameter. Drop into the boiling broth; cover tightly. Reduce heat to simmer, and cook 20 to 30 minutes. Makes 6 large servings.

Nutritional analysis per serving:

Calories 173, Fiber 3 gm, Cholesterol 35 mg, Sodium 1700 mg

% calories from:

Protein 12%, Carbohydrate 72%, Fat 16% (3 gm fat)

NOTE: To lower the sodium, make your matzo balls from scratch using matzo meal instead of the matzo mix. (the mix contains a lot of sodium).

Mushroom & Prosciutto Sauce With Pasta

Make this dish a complete dinner in one pan by tossing in 2 1/2 cups cooked vegetable of your choice!

1 Tbsp butter or margarine

3 cups mushrooms, sliced

6 green onions, chopped

2 to 3 cloves garlic, crushed or minced (or 1 tsp minced)

1/4 cup Madeira wine

4 oz sliced prosciutto, chopped

1 cup whole milk

1/2 cup freshly grated Parmesan cheese

Ground pepper to taste

5 cups cooked pasta noodles

224

Melt butter in a large nonstick skillet over medium-low heat. Add mushrooms, onions, and garlic, and sauté for about a minute. When it starts to get dry, add the wine, and stir. Continue cooking until mushrooms begin to brown. Add the prosciutto and cook for a minute, mixing well. Add the milk, and cook down slightly. Stir in Parmesan cheese and pepper. Add cooked pasta. Makes 5 servings.

Nutritional analysis per serving:

Calories 362, Fiber 3 gm, Cholesterol 40 mg, Sodium 646 mg

% calories from:

Protein 21%, Carbohydrate 51%, Fat 28% (11 gm fat)

Lemon-Broth Poached Salmon Steaks

Juice from 1 large or 2 small lemons

1/3 cup low-sodium chicken broth

2 salmon steaks or fillets (about 1/8 lb.)

Place lemon juice and chicken broth in medium sized covered saucepan. Add raw salmon steaks. Bring liquid to slow boil over medium-low heat. Reduce heat slightly, cover, and simmer 5 minutes. Flip salmon steaks over, cover, and continue to simmer 5 more minutes or until cooked throughout. Makes 2 servings.

NOTE: You can serve salmon over steamed rice and top with a tablespoon of poaching liquid.

Nutritional analysis per serving of salmon:

Calories 258, Fiber 0, Cholesterol 99 mg, Sodium 80 mg

% calories from:

Protein 58%, Carbohydrate 0%, Fat 42% (11.5 gm fat)

Oil-Free Salmon Fritters

1 egg yolk

2 Tbsp fat-free egg substitute

2 Tbsp flour

1/4 tsp salt

1/4 tsp dill weed

1/8 tsp pepper

1/2 tsp parsley flakes (or 1 tsp chopped parsley)

1 3/4 to 2 cups de-boned, de-skinned, and poached salmon
broken into very small pieces (use Lemon-Broth
Poached Salmon recipe on page 225; it makes exactly
this amount of flaked salmon). Canned salmon can be
used, but taste and saltiness may change significantly.

2 egg whites

No-stick cooking spray

Beat egg yolk with egg substitute in medium sized bowl until thick. Add flour, salt, dill, pepper, and parsley, and stir to blend. Stir salmon pieces into flour mixture. Beat egg whites until stiff. Fold them into salmon mixture. Coat a nonstick frying pan generously with no-stick cooking spray. Heat over medium heat. Remove pan from heat, and with a 1/4-cup measure, scoop 1/4 cup of fritter batter in pan. Repeat until pan is full. Place back on heat and continue to cook until bottom side is nicely browned, about 3 to 5 minutes. Turn to other side and cook until browned. Remove from pan. Coat pan again with no-stick spray for other fritters. Makes 3 servings (about 9 fritters).

Nutritional analysis per serving:

Calories 227, Fiber 0.1 gm, Cholesterol 137 mg, Sodium 288 mg

% calories from:

Protein 53%, Carbohydrate 8%, Fat 39% (9 gm fat)

NOTE: Fritters can be served with bread, rice, pasta, or Garlic-Parmesan Mayonnaise (recipe follows).

Garlic-Parmesan Mayonnaise:

1 tsp crushed or minced garlic (2-3 cloves garlic)

2 Tbsp shredded Parmesan cheese

1/2 tsp oregano flakes

1/4 cup reduced-fat mayonnaise

Blend ingredients together in small bowl. Makes about 4 servings of mayonnaise.

Nutritional analysis per serving:

Calories 35, Cholesterol 10 mg, Sodium 76 mg

% calories from:

Protein 17%, Carbohydrate 10%, Fat 74% (2.8 gm fat)

Low-Fat Glorified Chicken

4 skinless, boneless chicken breasts (about 1 1/2 lb)

1/4 cup white wine, chicken broth, or champagne

1 10 3/4-oz can Campbell's Healthy Request condensed cream of mushroom soup

2 cloves garlic, minced

1/8 teaspoon pepper

1/8 tsp crushed dried thyme, rosemary, or Italian seasoning

3 strips less-fat turkey bacon, cooked crisp and crumbled (optional)

No-stick cooking spray

Preheat oven to 375°. Coat the bottom half of a loaf pan generously with no-stick cooking spray. Arrange chicken in pan. Drizzle with wine or broth. Bake for 20 minutes. Combine condensed soup with garlic, pepper, and thyme. Spoon condensed soup mixture over chicken. Bake 30 minutes or until chicken is no longer pink. Sprinkle top with crumbled turkey bacon 10 minutes before cooking is completed, if desired. Stir sauce before serving. Makes 4 servings.

Nutritional analysis per serving:
Calories 185, Cholesterol 79 mg, Sodium 364 mg

% calories from:
Protein 62%, Carbohydrate 14%, Fat 24% (5 gm fat)

Pineapple Baked Beans (from scratch)

- 3 cups white beans, canned, drained (or cooked from dry)
- 1 Tbsp vinegar
- 3 Tbsp catsup
- 2 Tbsp prepared mustard
- 1 medium onion, chopped
- 1 8-oz can pineapple tidbits, drained
- 1/2 cup brown sugar, packed
- 2 Tbsp molasses
- 2 cloves garlic, minced or pressed (or 1/2 tsp garlic powder)
- 3 pieces less-fat Louis Rich turkey bacon, cooked crisp and crumbled (optional)

Preheat oven to 350°. Mix all ingredients together in 1 1/2 or 2 quart covered casserole. Bake for 45 minutes. Makes 6 servings.

229

Serving suggestion:

Serve with Bacon & Cheese Biscuits (recipe on page 106).

Nutritional analysis per serving:

Calories 255, Fiber 8 gm, Cholesterol 0, Sodium 171 mg

% calories from:

Protein 13%, Carbohydrate 84%, Fat 3% (1 gm fat)

Hearty Mexican Pizza

Crust:

1 Tbsp cornmeal

1 to 1 1/2 cups self-rising flour*, divided

1 cup whole wheat flour

3/4 cup beer, room temperature

2 Tbsp oil

2 Tbsp light sour cream

Topping:

1 16-oz can fat-free refried beans

1 lb ground sirloin (with no more than 12% fat)

1/2 cup chopped onion

1 1/4 cups tomato sauce or low-fat bottled spaghetti sauce

1 4-oz can chopped green chilies, undrained

2 cups shredded reduced-fat sharp cheddar, Monterey
  Jack, or mozzarella cheese

1 red or green bell pepper, cut into strips

Pitted ripe olives, sliced (optional)

Light sour cream (optional)

Taco or picante sauce (optional)

Preheat oven to 400°. Grease pizza pan or 15 x 10 x 1"
baking pan; sprinkle with cornmeal. In large bowl, combine 1/2 cup flour (measure by spooning the flour lightly
into measuring cup), whole wheat flour, beer, and oil; mix
well. Stir in 1/4 to 1/2 cup flour by hand to form a stiff
dough. On floured surface, knead in remaining 1/4 to 1/2
cup self-rising flour until dough is smooth and elastic, 2 to

3 minutes. Roll dough to 14" circle. Place over cornmeal in greased pan; press dough to fit pan evenly.

Spread beans over dough. In large skillet, brown ground beef. Add onion, tomato sauce, and chilies; blend well. Spoon meat mixture over refried beans; top with cheese, pepper strips, and olives. Bake for 25 to 35 minutes or until crust is light golden brown. Let stand 5 minutes before serving. Garnish with sour cream or taco sauce. Makes 8 servings.

Nutritional analysis per serving:
Calories 384, Fiber 7 gm, Cholesterol 54 mg, Sodium 982 mg

% calories from:
Protein 29%, Carbohydrate 48%, Fat 23% (10 gm fat)

* All-purpose or unbleached flour can be substituted for self-rising flour; add 2 tsp baking powder and 1/2 tsp salt.

Tomato Swiss Steak

1/4 cup flour

1/4 tsp pepper

1 lb round steak (3/4" thick)

1 tsp canola oil, or other vegetable oil

1 11-oz can Campbell's condensed tomato bisque soup

1/2 cup beer, wine, or water

1 cup sliced onions

1 tsp Worcestershire sauce (or low-sodium soy sauce)

3 carrots, sliced

3 stalks celery, sliced

No-stick cooking spray

Blend flour with pepper. Pound as much flour as possible into steak(s). Cut steak into serving-size pieces if it's not already cut. Coat a large nonstick skillet generously with no-stick cooking spray, then place oil in skillet. Brown steak in oil. Add remaining ingredients. Stir gently, and cover. Cook over low heat about 1 to 1 1/2 hours or until done. Stir occasionally. Serve with mashed potatoes, rice, or noodles. Makes 4 to 6 servings.

Nutritional analysis per serving (if 4 servings per recipe):

Calories 241, Fiber 4.3 gm, Cholesterol 98 mg, Sodium 707 mg

% calories from:

Protein 38%, Carbohydrate 39%, Fat 26% (9.5 gm fat)

232

Summer Savory Rice
(with sausage & squash)

6 oz light sausage (e.g., Jimmy Dean light sausage)

1 yellow onion, chopped

3 cloves garlic, minced or pressed

2/3 cup white wine, light or nonalcoholic beer, or low-sodium broth, divided

4 ripe tomatoes, chopped

3/4 tsp sage

1 tsp oregano leaves

3 cups cooked or steamed rice

2 cups coarsely chopped summer squash, microwaved or steamed

Pepper to taste

Start to cook sausage in a large saucepan or covered skillet over medium-low heat. Add in onion and garlic, and cook for a couple minutes, crumbling sausage into small pieces as it cooks. Add in 1/3 cup of the wine or broth and continue to cook, stirring frequently, until sausage is browned and onion is just tender. Stir in remaining wine, tomatoes, sage, and oregano; reduce heat to simmer, and cook for 10 minutes. Stir in rice and squash, and pepper to taste. Simmer for a couple of minutes to blend flavors. Makes 4 servings.

233

Nutritional analysis per serving:

Calories 393, Fiber 4.3 gm, Cholesterol 34 mg, Sodium 313 mg

% calories from:

Protein 17%, Carbohydrate 61%, Fat 22% (9.8 gm fat)

Cheese Pie

2 eggs

3/4 cup flour

1 cup milk, divided

2 cups finely chopped broccoli (or carrots, cauliflower, spinach, or other vegetables in season)

1/2 cup finely chopped zucchini (or green peppers or other vegetables in season)

4 to 5 oz reduced-fat sharp cheddar cheese, grated

1 small onion, finely chopped

1 tsp parsley flakes

1 tsp basil flakes

1 tsp garlic, minced or pressed

Parmesan cheese (optional)

No-stick cooking spray

234

Preheat oven to 425°. Beat eggs well in mixing bowl. Add flour. Pour in 1/2 cup of the milk and blend well. Let the batter sit while you cut up the vegetables. Coat a 9 x 9" glass baking pan (glass makes a better crust) with no-stick cooking spray. Spread the broccoli and zucchini evenly over the bottom of pan. Sprinkle the cheddar cheese over the top, then top the cheese with the onion. Now, go back to the batter. Add in the parsley, basil, and garlic and beat in the remaining milk. Pour this mixture over the vegetables and cheese. Sprinkle Parmesan over the top if you desire. Bake for about 25 minutes or until golden. Makes 6 servings.

Nutritional analysis per serving:

Calories 177, Fiber 2 gm, Cholesterol 83 mg, Sodium 163 mg

% calories from:

Protein 28%, Carbohydrate 42%, Fat 30% (6 gm fat)

Salad For Supper

You are finally home from work and you open all the windows and doors in the house, but you still can't feel a breeze blowing in. You try to cool off with a tall glass of iced tea, and the thought of turning on the oven or microwave sounds oppressive. Right place—wrong appliances.

Instead, consider reaching in the refrigerator for a cool, crisp Chinese chicken salad smothered in tangy sesame dressing or a tender chilled tortellini pasta salad, featuring colorful summer vegetables, dressed with a piquant vinaigrette. Or picture yourself biting into a taco salad, with tender, spicy beef, tangy tomatoes, sharp cheddar cheese, and crunchy tortilla chips. These are all salads you can serve for supper on a warm summer day and hit most of the major food groups.

But all three of these main dish salads can pack quite a load of calories and fat. Here are some specific tips on how to lighten up your Chinese chicken, taco, and entree pasta salads, along with recipes to get you started.

235

Chinese Chicken Salad Tips

- Say "no" to fried rice noodles and save yourself from all that extra oil

- Grill or broil the skinless chicken breasts (don't deep fry or stir-fry) to cut about 2 teaspoons of oil the chicken would have absorbed. Slice each grilled breast diagonally for decorative strips of chicken.

- Sprinkle 2 tablespoons of sliced almonds over the salad instead of 1/3 cup or more. To make the most of a little bit of nuts, sprinkle the almonds on top of each serving instead of mixing them into the salad.

- Since crispiness in this Chinese chicken salad is lacking (due to a decrease in nuts and the elimination of crispy fried noodles), you may want to use iceberg lettuce as your salad green of choice.

Dressing Tips:

Replace the 1/4 cup of oil normally called for with orange or apple juice (for maximum flavor use freshly squeezed orange juice), but keep the 1 tablespoon of sesame oil (it contributes an irreplaceable flavor).

Chinese Chicken Salad

4 skinless chicken breast halves

1 head iceberg lettuce, shredded

1/4 cup sliced green onions with tops

1/3 cup cilantro leaves (optional)

2 Tbsp toasted sliced almonds

1 Tbsp toasted sesame seeds (optional)

Dressing:

1 Tbsp milk or low-sodium soy sauce

1/4 cup orange juice (freshly squeezed if possible)

2 Tbsp sugar

1 Tbsp sesame oil

3 Tbsp rice vinegar

Grill or broil chicken breasts, basting with orange juice or low-sodium chicken broth. Cut diagonally to make decorative strips. Toss with lettuce, onions, and cilantro leaves if desired. Mix dressing ingredients in small bowl until blended (makes about 1/2 cup). Pour dressing over salad ingredients and toss. Dish each serving onto a dinner plate. Sprinkle each serving with toasted almonds and sesame seeds. Makes 4 servings.

237

Nutritional analysis per serving:

Calories 247, Fiber 2 gm, Cholesterol 73 mg, Sodium 200 mg

% calories from:

Protein 47%, Carbohydrate 19%, Fat 34% (9 gm fat)

Taco Salad Tips

- Use 8 ounces of tortilla chips (about half of a 1-pound bag) instead of 14 ounces. Some of the fat in taco salads comes from the chips. To cut some fat without giving up all the crunchiness, just use less. Of course, fat-free tortilla chips are available in most supermarkets. If you are going to use these, buy the kind with salt (you'll need the flavor) and add the chips just as you are about to eat (the chips without grease get soggy faster).

- Use a reduced-fat sharp cheddar cheese instead of the regular 9 grams of fat per ounce type of cheddar. Kraft Light Naturals and Cracker Barrel Light both make excellent tasting lower-fat sharp cheddars.

- Use the leanest ground beef you can find, such as 91% fat-free ground sirloin. If there is a ground turkey breast product you like that is also around 91% fat-free, by all means, use that too.

238

- Since we're adding fewer chips, we can bulk up our taco salad by mixing in a can of drained kidney beans (no-salt-added varieties are available in most supermarkets).

Dressing Tips:

Just 1 cup of mayo adds 160 grams of fat and 1,600 calories. Trim down the fat to 40 grams without cutting out the flavor by using 1/2 cup of light mayo and 1/2 cup of nonfat Knudsen free sour cream. (Or cut out the fat completely by trying the new nonfat mayonnaise.)

Taco Salad

1 lb very lean ground sirloin

1/2 envelope Lawry's taco seasoning

8 oz reduced-fat sharp cheddar cheese, grated

1 head iceberg lettuce, shredded

3 tomatoes, diced

1 sweet or mild onion, chopped

1 15-oz can kidney beans, drained

Sliced black olives (optional)

8 oz. tortilla chips (less-salt if available)

Dressing:

1/2 cup light mayonnaise (or fat-free if desired)

1/2 cup fat-free sour cream

4-8 oz Pace Picante mild salsa (or similar)

Brown meat with seasoning until cooked throughout and nicely browned. In large bowl, toss seasoned beef with grated cheese, shredded lettuce, tomatoes, onion, and beans. Add sliced olives if desired. In small bowl, blend dressing ingredients. Add chips and dressing to salad ingredients right before serving. Makes 8 large servings.

(239)

Nutritional analysis per serving:

Calories 405, Fiber 7 gm, Cholesterol 61 mg, Sodium varies according to salsa and seasoning

% calories from:

Protein 28%, Carbohydrate 32%, Fat 40% (19 gm fat)
NOTE: The original recipe contained 723 calories, 92 mg cholesterol and 55 gm fat!

Chef Salad Tips

- Chef salad is usually offered with your choice of dressing but is often served with ranch dressing (about 8 grams of fat per tablespoon).

- The typical chef salad, made with tomatoes, strips of ham, turkey, and cheese, boiled egg halves, and ranch dressing all over a mound of iceberg lettuce contains about 500 calories, 68% calories from fat (38 grams of fat) and 305 milligrams of cholesterol. But top that same mound of lettuce with boiled egg white, tomatoes, 2 ounces of reduced-fat cheese, an ounce each of a very lean ham and turkey breast cold cut, and 1/4 cup of reduced-fat ranch dressing (e.g., Hidden Valley Ranch packet made with 1 1/2 cups 1% low-fat milk, 1/4 cup fat-free sour cream, and 1/4 cup light mayonnaise), and the nutritional picture brightens—333 calories, 14.5 grams of fat (37% calories from fat) and 80 milligrams of cholesterol.

Crab or Shrimp Louie Tips

• The dressing for crab or shrimp Louie is generally Thousand Island with about 8 grams of fat per tablespoon.

• Crab and shrimp are both low in fat (although shrimp is a bit high in cholesterol compared to other seafood), and so are tomatoes and lettuce. The only other item that adds fat is the boiled egg, which is quartered and used as garnish. One serving of this type of Shrimp Louie salad can total 360 calories, 25 grams of fat, and 260 milligrams of cholesterol. If you garnish the salad with hard boiled egg white and use low-fat Thousand Island dressing (see recipe below), the figures fall to 120 calories, 2 to 3 grams of fat, and 140 milligrams of cholesterol.

Thousand Island Dressing:
1/4 cup light mayonnaise

1/4 cup fat-free mayonnaise

2 Tbsp catsup

1-2 Tbsp minced stuffed olives or dill pickles

1 Tbsp minced onion

2 tsp parsley flakes

1/2 Tbsp chopped green pepper (optional)

1/2 hard-cooked egg, chopped (optional)

Combine the above ingredients and serve over salad greens. Makes about 3/4 cup of dressing.

Nutritional analysis per 2 Tbsp serving:
Calories 54, Fiber 3 gm, Cholesterol 3 mg, Sodium 300 mg

% calories from:
Protein 1%, Carbohydrate 44%, Fat 55% (3 gm fat)

241

Taking it
a Week at a Time—

A Sample Week Using Recipes From This Book

The traditional meal pattern for most people is to eat two or three meals a day, with the largest meal at the end of the day. This book is devoted to helping you shift from this potentially destructive way of eating to eating small, frequent meals throughout the day and eating light at night—a meal pattern that matches your metabolism more precisely. To help you do this, tables listing the better choices in many of the most popular snack categories were included in this book along with recipes for snacks and lighter meals.

But how do all these pieces fit together? What does the total picture look like? That's what this sample week will show you. I used slightly less than the Recommended Daily Allowance (RDA) for women age 19 to 50 (2,000 calories versus the RDA of 2,200) and men (2,700 versus the RDA of 2,900) as my calorie guide for each day. (Remember, RDAs are average figures, some people may actually need more while others need less.)

Using the sample week, you'll be able to see how various recipes in this book, put together with other food items, add up over a day.

There are several ways to eat small, frequent meals throughout the day. One way is to eat five or so equally portioned small meals with all contributing about the same calories. Another way is to eat three definite meals—a light breakfast, lunch, and dinner—with two or so snacks in between. I have a bias toward the latter just because that's how I've eaten for the past 10 years. I also think it's the most practical way to go for many of us who work, are raising children, or have been in the habit of only eating two or three large meals over the day. But both ways of eating light are reflected in the sample week (see Day 5 and 6 for examples of eating equally portioned small meals).

Day 1

Total of 2,000 calories	Calories	Fat gm
Breakfast		
Whole wheat cinnamon toast, 2 slices	237	8.7
8 oz orange juice	102	0.4
2 strips Louis Rich turkey bacon	60	5
Decaf latte made with skim milk (1/2 cup)	45	0
Total (28% calories from fat)	**444**	**14.1**
Snack		
1 packet instant oatmeal (bran with raisin) made with nonfat milk (2/3 cup)		
Total (10% calories from fat)	**240**	**2.6**

Day 1 Continued

Total of 2,000 calories	Calories	Fat gm
Lunch		
The 3-Minute Burrito	433	14
1 apple and a carrot cut into sticks	156	0.9
Total **589**		**14.9**
(23% calories from fat)		
Snack		
1 oz less-salt pretzels	113	1
2 reduced-fat Vienna Fingers sandwich cookies	130	3.5
Total **243**		**4.5**
(17% calories from fat)		
Dinner		
Deluxe Chicken Noodle Soup, 1 serving (contains vegetables)	176	5.5
1 dinner roll	120	3
1/2 cup light vanilla ice cream	100	4
with 1/2 cup fresh or frozen berries	33	0.2
Total **429**		**12.7**
(27% calories from fat)		

(245)

**Total for the day—
1,945 calories, 49 gm fat
(23% calories from fat)**

Day 2

Total of 2,700 calories	Calories	Fat gm

Breakfast

	Calories	Fat gm
1 serving of Light Denver Omelette For Two with 2 pieces of whole wheat toast and jam or preserves	388	10
1 cup cantaloupe cubes	56	0.5
2 pieces turkey breakfast sausage	130	9
8 oz orange juice	102	0.4
Total (26% calories from fat)	**676**	**19.9**

Snack

	Calories	Fat gm
2 Chocolate Zucchini Muffins		
Total (20% calories from fat)	**320**	**7**

Lunch

	Calories	Fat gm
2 Tuna and Tartar Salad Sandwiches	614	11.2
Green salad with cucumber, tomato, broccoli, and 2 Tbsp reduced-calorie Italian dressing	100	6
Total (22% calories from fat)	**714**	**17.2**

Day 2 Continued

Total of 2,700 calories	Calories	Fat gm

Snack

	Calories	Fat gm
Creamy Lemon Pie, 1 serving	202	5
8 oz 1% low-fat milk	96	2.2
Total	**298**	**7.2**
(22% calories from fat)		

Dinner

	Calories	Fat gm
Superior Meatloaf and Potatoes	502	10
3/4 cup apple compote with cinnamon-sugar (or lightly sweetened applesauce with cinnamon)	113	0.8
Total	**615**	**10.8**
(16% calories from fat)		

**Total for the day—
2,635 calories, 62 gm fat
(21% calories from fat)**

Day 3

Total of 2,000 calories	Calories	Fat gm
Breakfast		
Lemon Scone	303	6.5
1 cup strawberries	22	0.3
8 oz orange juice	102	0.4
Total 427 (15% calories from fat)		**7.2**

Snack		
6 oz low-fat fruit flavored yogurt mixed with 1/3 cup Grapenuts or low-fat granola	307	2
Total 307 (6% calories from fat)		**2**

Lunch		
Fish Sandwich	380	14.5
1 banana	132	0.7
Vegetable sticks (1/2 carrot, 1/2 cup zucchini, 1/2 celery stalk, cut into sticks) plus 1 1/2 Tbsp reduced-fat peanut butter	142	9
Total 654 (33% calories from fat)		**24.2**

Day 3 Continued
Total of 2,000 calories

	Calories	Fat gm
Snack		
Iced Cafe Mocha	186	2.7
2 whole graham crackers (cinnamon or regular)	60	1.5
Total (15% calories from fat)	**246**	**4.2**

	Calories	Fat gm
Dinner		
Artichoke Heart & Bacon Fettuccini	310	9.5
Whole wheat dinner roll with 1 tsp diet margarine	120	5
Total (30% calories from fat)	**430**	**14.5**

Total for the day—
2,064 calories, 51.7 gm fat
(23% calories from fat)

249

Day 4
Total of 2,700 calories

	Calories	Fat gm
Breakfast		
2 Raspberry Whole Wheat Muffins	432	7.6
Hot cocoa made with 1 cup of nonfat milk	150	1
1 cup fruit salad	82	0.5
Total (12% calories from fat)	**664**	**9.1**
Snack		
Bagel With Herb & Onion Spread	262	6
1 orange spritzer (made with 6 oz orange juice and 6 oz club soda, diet 7-Up, or sparkling mineral water)	76	0.3
Total (17% calories from fat)	**338**	**6.3**
Lunch		
Fast Chili Nachos with 1 1/2 oz restaurant style white corn Tostitos	602	21.5
1 cup low-fat frozen yogurt	220	3.5
Total (27% calories from fat)	**822**	**25**

Day 4 Continued
Total of 2,700 calories

	Calories	Fat gm

Snack

	Calories	Fat gm
1 Christmas Quesadilla	206	7.8
1 cup of grapes	113	0.9
Total	**319**	**8.7**
(25% calories from fat)		

Dinner

	Calories	Fat gm
Pork Tenderloin Florentine (including rice)	422	12
3/4 cup sliced peaches topped with gingersnap cookie crumbs (about 2 cookies, crumbled)	160	3
Total	**582**	**15**
(23% calories from fat)		

Total for the day—
2,725 calories, 64 gm fat
(21% calories from fat)

251

Fight Fat and Win Light Meals and Snacks

Day 5
Total of 2,000 calories

	Calories	Fat gm
Breakfast		
Strawberry-Filled French Toast	285	4
1 cup cantaloupe cubes	56	0.5
1 cup 1% low-fat milk	102	2.5
Total **443** (14% calories from fat)		**7**
Snack		
2 granola bars (e.g., Nature Valley low-fat chewy chocolate chip)	240	4
8 oz orange juice	102	0.4
Total **342** (12% calories from fat)		**4.4**
Lunch		
Cold Country Oven Fried Chicken	258	6.6
German Potato Salad	194	2
Total **452** (17% calories from fat)		**8.6**

Day 5 Continued

Total of 2,000 calories	Calories	Fat gm

Snack

	Calories	Fat gm
Glorified Grilled Cheese	275	9
3/4 cup each raw broccoli and cauliflower florets with 1 Tbsp regular ranch dressing for dipping (or 2-3 Tbsp reduced calorie)	91	5.9
1 apple	125	0.7
Total **491** (29% calories from fat)		**15.6**

Dinner

	Calories	Fat gm
Grilled Fish With Light Mustard Sauce	228	6
1/2 cup steamed rice mixed with 1/2 cup steamed carrot coins	167	0.4
Total **395** (15% calories from fat)		**6.4**

Total for the day—
2,125 calories, 40 gm fat
(17% calories from fat)

253

Day 6
Total of 2,700 calories

	Calories	Fat gm
Breakfast		
Oil-Free Potato Pancakes, 2 servings (about 6 small pancakes)	282	3.6
3 slices Canadian style bacon, pan-fried (with no-stick cooking spray)	130	5.9
8 oz orange juice	102	0.4
Total (18% calories from fat)	**514**	**9.9**
Snack		
1 1/2 cups Raisin Bran cereal with 3/4 cup 2% low-fat milk	347	5
3 fig bars	150	3
Total (14% calories from fat)	**497**	**8**
Lunch		
Light Club Sandwich	404	10.8
6 oz low-fat flavored yogurt	173	2
Total (20% calories from fat)	**577**	**12.8**

Day 6 Continued

Total of 2,700 Calories	Calories	Fat gm
Snack		
Quick Fix Chili and Fries	500	10
Total	**500**	**10**
(18% calories from fat)		

Dinner		
Chicken Cream Cheese Rolls	251	10.5
3/4 cup steamed rice	198	0.4
1 cup green beans	44	0.4
1 cup Fruit Salad With Raspberry Orange Dressing	173	0.3
Total	**666**	**11.6**
(16% calories from fat)		

Total for the day —
2,754 calories, 52 gm fat
(17% calories from fat)

255

Day 7

Total of 2,000 calories	Calories	Fat gm
Breakfast		
Apple Lover's Oatmeal	225	1.6
2 pieces whole wheat toast with 2 tsp diet margarine	213	8.7
1 cup 1% low-fat milk	104	2.4
Total 542 (21% calories from fat)		**12.7**

	Calories	Fat gm
Snack		
1 slice Banana Rum Raisin Bread	299	4
Total 299 (12% calories from fat)		**4**

	Calories	Fat gm
Lunch		
BBQ Pork Sandwich	381	6.4
3/4 cup steamed broccoli florets with 1 oz reduced-fat sharp cheddar melted over it	112	5.3
1 orange	64	0.1
Total 557 (19% calories from fat)		**11.8**

Day 7 Continued

Total of 2,000 calories	Calories	Fat gm

Snack

4 cups air-popped (or use no-oil microwave popper) popcorn with 2 tsp butter or margarine and butter sprinkles	191	9.3

	Total	191	9.3
	(44% calories from fat)		

Dinner

10-minute Ravioli With Marinara	294	10
1 cup steamed zucchini	30	0.1
2 pumpkin spice cookies	168	3.4

Total	492	13.5
(25% calories from fat)		

Total for the day—
2,081 calories, 51 gm fat
(22% calories from fat)

Index

3-Minute Microwave Chili Dog, 147
10-Minute Ravioli With Marinara, 184

Apple Butter Mini Spice Cakes, 108-109
Apple Lover's Oatmeal, 138
apple breakfast tart, caramel, 104-105
apple cake, quick, 94-95
Apricot Rum Raisin Rice Pudding, 88-89
Artichoke Heart and Bacon Fettuccini, 189

Bacon & Cheese Biscuits, 106-107
Bacon & Cheese Muffins, 128-129
bacon fettuccini, artichoke heart and, 189
Bagel & Egg Sandwich, 114
bagel
    chips, oil-free, 76
    spread,
        herb & onion, 135
        lox-ness monster, 136
        sun-dried tomato-pesto, 134
baked beans, pineapple, 229
Banana Rum Raisin Bread, 130-131
banana, peanut butter, 57
barbecue chicken in winter, 202-203
Barbecued Pork Sandwiches, 154-155
BBQ Chicken in Winter, 202-203
bean enchiladas, four-can beef &, 200-201
beans,
    one-pot Mexican rice &, 180-181
    pineapple baked, 229
beef & bean enchiladas, four-can, 200-201
Biscuit Pan Pizza, 148-149
biscuit
    blanket, hot dogs in a, 211
    pie, chicken curry, 212-213
biscuits, bacon & cheese, 106-107
blood glucose and eating, 4
bread,
    banana rum raisin, 130-131
    cheese, 64
    cranberry-oat orange, 120

breakfast, 10, 25, 33-34, 102-139
burrito, the 3-minute, 146

Cabbage Rolls, 194-195
cake,
    quick apple, 94-95
    sock-it-to-me coffee, 126-127
cakes, apple butter mini spice, 108-109
California Roll Sushi, 174-175
calories, distribution of, 26
Caramel Apple Breakfast Tart, 104-105
Caramel Corn, 60
caramel
    nut crust, 91
    sauce, light, 105
caramels, less-fat, 100
casserole,
    easy ham & potato, 198
    meat & potato, 220-221
cereal, 42-46
Cheese Bread, 64
Cheese Pie, 234
cheese
    biscuits, bacon &, 106-107
    fondue, microwave, 63
    muffins, bacon &, 128-129
cheese, 37-38
    glorified grilled, 166
    pintos and, 79
cheesecake,
    chocolate lovers', 98-99
    Kahlua white Russian, 90
Chef Salad, 240-241
cherry
    frozen yogurt, chocolate-covered, 69
    wink cookies, light, 96-97
Chicken Cream Cheese Rolls, 196-197
Chicken Curry Biscuit Pie, 212-213
Chicken Nachos, 164
chicken
    & pork with peanut sauce, Indonesian style, 214-215
    in winter, BBQ, 202-203
    noodle salad, Japanese, 176-177
    noodle soup, deluxe, 173
    salad sandwich with dill dressing, smoked, 165
chicken,
    cold country oven fried, 156-157

low-fat glorified, 228
moist microwave, 188
chili and fries, quick-fix, 152
chili dog, 3-minute microwave, 147
chili nachos, fast, 163
Chinese Chicken Salad, 236-237
chips, 41-42
oil-free bagel, 76
Chocolate and Peanut Butter Ice
Milk, 66
Chocolate Cookie Crust, 98
Chocolate Filling, 99
Chocolate Lovers' Cheesecake, 98-99
Chocolate Mint Cookies, 86-87
Chocolate Zucchini Muffins, 116-117
chocolate
malt, old fashioned, 70
oatmeal chippers, light, 84
Chocolate-Covered Cherry Frozen
Yogurt, 69
Christmas Quesadilla, 78
cinnamon toast, whole wheat, 115
club sandwich, light, 167
coffee cake, sock-it-to-me, 126-127
Cold Country Oven Fried Chicken,
156-157
cookies, 48-50
chocolate mint, 86-87
light cherry wink cookies, 96-97
light chocolate oatmeal chippers,
84
pumpkin spice, 92-93
Crab Louie salad, 241
crab crepes, quick, 206-207
Cracker Bag Snack, 75
crackers, 38-40
Cranberry-Oat Orange Bread, 120
cream cheese rolls, chicken, 196-197
Creamy Lemon Pie, 82
Creamy Rum Topping, 98
crepes,
no-cholesterol, 207
quick crab, 206-207
Crispix mix, low-fat, 73

Croque Monsieur, 153
crudités and crackers, spicy hummus with, 160-161
crust,
caramel nut, 91
chocolate cookie, 98
graham cracker, 83
curry biscuit pie, chicken, 212-213

Deluxe Chicken Noodle Soup, 173
Deluxe Ramen Oriental Soup, 172
Denver omelette for two, light, 102-103
desserts, 82-100
diet plans, 13, 16-19, 243-257
digestion, 5
dill dressing, smoked chicken salad
sandwich with, 165
Dinner Pancakes, 219
dinner, 6-7, 8-9, 29-30, 172-241
dip,
fruity fruit, 53
quick ranch, 55
dressing, smoked chicken salad
sandwich with dill, 165

Easy Ham & Potato Casserole, 198
Egg Muffin Lite, 110-111
Egg Salad Sandwiches, 162
egg sandwich, bagel &, 114
enchiladas, four-can beef & bean,
200-201
espresso ice cream, oreo, 68
exercise, 7-8

Fast Chili Nachos, 163
fat, distribututions of dietary, 27
fettuccini, artichoke heart and bacon,
189
filling, chocolate, 99
Fish Sandwich, 150-151
fish with light mustard sauce,
grilled, 218
florentine, pork tenderloin, 190-191
fondue, microwave cheese, 63

food groups, 12
Four-Can Beef & Bean Enchiladas, 200-201
French toast, strawberry-filled, 124-125
fried rice, quick-fix, 144-145
fries, quick-fix chili and, 152
frittata, zucchini-tomato, 112-113
fritters, oil-free salmon, 226-227
frozen yogurt, lemon drop, 67
Fruity Fruit Dip, 53

Garlic-Parmesan Mayonnaise, 227
German Potato Salad, 186-187
glaze, maple, 109
Glorified Grilled Cheese, 166
glorified chicken, low-fat, 228
graham cracker crust, 83
Granola Snack Bars, 74
granola parfait, yogurt, 59
grazing, 4-6
Grilled Fish With Light Mustard Sauce, 218
grilled cheese, glorified, 166

ham & potato casserole, easy, 198
ham and Swiss sandwich, 153
Hearty Mexican Pizza, 230-231
heavy eating, 1
Herb & Onion Bagel Spread, 135
Herb-Roasted Pork Tenderloin, 209
Herb-Roasted Potatoes, 210
Hot Dogs in a Biscuit Blanket, 211
hot dog, 3-minute microwave chili, 147
hummus with crudités and crackers, spicy, 160-161

ice cream, 46-48
    light tin roof sundae, 85
    oreo-espresso, 68
ice milk, chocolate and peanut butter, 66
Iced Cafe Mocha, 77

Indonesian Style Chicken & Pork With Peanut Sauce, 214-215

Japanese Chicken Noodle Salad, 176-177
julliette, orange, 52

Kahlua White Russian Cheesecake, 90
krispy treats, peanut butter, 56

lasagna, no more boil vegetable, 216-217
late-night snacks, 82-100
Lemon Drop Frozen Yogurt, 67
Lemon Scones, 122-123
Lemon Zucchini Muffins, 137
lemon pie, creamy, 82
Lemon-Broth Poached Salmon Steaks, 225
Less-Fat Caramels, 100
Light Caramel Sauce, 105
Light Cherry Wink Cookies, 96-97
Light Chocolate Oatmeal Chippers, 84
Light Club Sandwich, 167
Light Denver Omelette for Two, 102-103
Light Tartar Sauce, 151
Light Tin Roof Sundae, 85
light foods, defined, 2
light meals, benefits of, 4-7
Loop De Loop Snack, 72
Low-Fat Crispix Mix, 73
Low-Fat Glorified Chicken, 228
low-fat diets, 2-4
Lox-Ness Monster Bagel Spread, 136
lunch, 11, 142-169

malt, old fashioned chocolate, 70
Mandarin Orange Sorbet, 65
Maple Glaze, 109
marinara, 10-minute ravioli with, 184
matzo ball soup, quick less-fat vegetable, 222-223

mayonnaise, garlic-Parmesan, 227
meal patterns, 22-29
meal size, 1, 22, 24-31
    determining, 14-15
Meat & Potato Casserole, 220-221
meatloaf and potatoes, superior, 178-179
menopause, 5
menu plans, 13, 16-19, 243-257
metabolism, 5, 21
Mexican pizza, hearty, 230-231
Mexican rice & beans, one-pot, 180-181
Mexican-Style Potato, 142
Microwave Cheese Fondue, 63
Microwave Zucchini Summer Soup, 182-183
microwave
    chicken, moist, 188
    chili dog, 3-minute, 147
mini spice cakes, apple butter, 108-109
mint cookies, chocolate, 86-87
mix,
    low-fat Crispix, 73
    trail, 71
Moist (and Low-fat) Microwave Chicken, 188
Monte Cristo Sandwich, 168-169
mousse, strawberry-yogurt, 58
muffin lite, egg, 110-111
muffins,
    bacon & cheese, 128-129
    chocolate zucchini, 116-117
    lemon zucchini, 137
    raspberry whole wheat, 118-119
Mushroom & Prosciutto Sauce With Pasta, 224
mustard sauce, grilled gish with light, 218

nachos,
    chicken, 164
    fast chili, 163
nighttime snacking, 6-7, 9-10, 29-30, 34

No More Boil Vegetable Lasagna, 216-217
No-Cholesterol Crepes, 207
nutrients, distribution of, 28

oatmeal chippers, light chocolate, 84
oatmeal, apple lover's, 138
Oil-Free Bagel Chips, 76
Oil-Free Potato Pancakes, 132-133
Oil-Free Salmon Fritters, 226-227
Old Fashioned Chocolate Malt, 70
omelette for two, light Denver, 102-103
One-Pot Mexican Rice & Beans, 180-181
onion bagel spread, herb &, 135
Orange Julliette, 52
orange
    bread, cranberry-oat, 120
    sorbet, mandarin, 65
Oreo-Espresso Ice Cream, 68
oriental soup, deluxe Ramen, 172
oven fried chicken, cold country, 156-157

pan pizza, biscuit, 148-149
pancakes,
    dinner, 219
    oil-free potato, 132-133
    peanut butter, 121
parfait, yogurt granola, 59
Parmesan Popcorn, 62
pasta, mushroom & prosciutto sauce with, 224
Peanut Butter Banana, 57
Peanut Butter Krispy Treats, 56
Peanut Butter Pancakes, 121
Peanut Butter Vegetable Spread, 54
peanut butter ice milk, chocolate and, 66
peanut butter, 38
peanut sauce, Indonesian style chicken & pork with, 214-215
pesto, sun-dried tomato, 108
pie crust, graham cracker, 83

pie,
  cheese, 234
  chicken curry biscuit, 212-213
  creamy lemon, 82-83
Pineapple Baked Beans, 229
Pintos and Cheese, 79
Pizza Potato, 143
pizza,
  biscuit pan, 148-149
  hearty Mexican, 230-231
PMS, 5
poached salmon steaks, lemon-broth, 225
popcorn, 37
  caramel, 60
  Parmesan, 62
Pork Tenderloin Florentine, 190-191
pork
  sandwiches, barbecued, 154-155
  tenderloin, herb-roasted, 209
  with peanut sauce, Indonesian style chicken &, 214-215
  with rice, sweet and sour, 204-205
portion sizes, 9
potato
  casserole, easy ham &, 198
  casserole, meat &, 220-221
  pancakes, oil-free, 132-133
  salad, German, 186-187
potato,
  Mexican-style, 142
  pizza, 143
potatoes,
  herb-roasted, 210
  superior meatloaf and, 178-179
premenstrual syndrome (PMS), 5
prosciutto sauce with pasta, mushroom &, 224
pudding, apricot rum raisin rice, 88-89
Pumpkin Spice Cookies, 92-93

quesadilla, Christmas, 78
Quick Apple Cake, 94-95
Quick Crab Crepes, 206-207

Quick Less-Fat Vegetable Matzo Ball Soup, 222-223
Quick Ranch Dip, 55
Quick Tortellini Soup, 185
Quick-Fix Chili and Fries, 152
Quick-Fix Fried Rice, 144-145

raisin bread, banana rum, 130-131
Ramen oriental soup, deluxe, 172
ranch dip, quick, 55
Raspberry Whole Wheat Muffins, 118-119
ravioli with marinara, 10-minute, 184
rice & beans, one-pot Mexican, 180-181
rice pudding, apricot rum raisin, 88-89
rice,
  quick-fix fried, 144-145
  summer savory, 233
  sweet and sour pork with, 204-205
risotto, seafood, 192-193
rolls,
  cabbage, 194-195
  chicken cream cheese, 196-197
rum topping, creamy, 98

salad,
  German potato, 186-187
  Japanese chicken noodle, 176-177
  tuna & tartar, 158-159
salads tips, 235-241
salmon
  fritters, oil-free, 226-227
  steaks,
  lemon-broth poached, 225
  spicy, 199
sample meals, 243-257
sandwich with dill dressing, smoked chicken salad, 165
sandwich,
  bagel & egg, 114
  croque monsieur, 153
  fish, 150-151
  light club, 167
  Monte Cristo, 168-169

sandwiches,
  barbecued pork, 154-155
  egg salad, 162
sauce,
  light caramel, 105
  light tartar, 151
  tartar, 158
savory rice, summer, 233
scones, lemon, 122-123
scramble, vegetable, 139
Seafood Risotto, 192-193
Shrimp Louie salad, 241
Smoked Chicken Salad Sandwich
  With Dill Dressing, 165
snack bars, granola, 74
snack,
  cracker bag, 75
  loop de loop, 72
snacks, 33-50, 52-79
  most popular, 35
Sock-It-to-Me Coffee Cake, 126-127
sorbet, mandarin orange, 65
soup,
  deluxe chicken noodle, 173
  deluxe Ramen oriental, 172
  microwave zucchini summer,
    182-183
  quick less-fat vegetable matzo ball,
    222-223
  quick tortellini, 185
spice
  cakes, apple butter mini, 108-109
  cookies, pumpkin, 92-93
Spicy Hummus With Crudités and
  Crackers, 160-161
Spicy Salmon Steaks, 199
spread,
  herb & onion bagel, 135
  lox-ness monster bagel, 136
  peanut butter vegetable, 54
  sun-dried tomato-pesto bagel, 134
steak, tomato Swiss, 232
steaks, spicy salmon, 199
Strawberry-Filled French Toast,
  124-125
Strawberry-Yogurt Mousse, 58

Summer Savory Rice, 233
Sun-Dried Tomato Pesto, 108
Sun-Dried Tomato-Pesto Bagel
  Spread, 134
sundae, light tin roof, 85
Superior Meatloaf and Potatoes,
  178-179
sushi, California roll, 174-175
Sweet and Sour Pork With Rice,
  204-205
Swiss steak, tomato, 232

Taco Salad, 238-239
tart, caramel apple breakfast, 104-
  105
Tartar Sauce, 158
tartar
  salad, tuna &, 158-159
  sauce, light, 151
tenderloin florentine, pork, 190-191
tenderloin, herb-roasted pork, 209
The 3-Minute Burrito, 146
tin roof sundae, light, 85
toast, whole wheat cinnamon, 115
Tomato Swiss Steak, 232
tomato
  frittata, zucchini, 112-113
  pesto, sun-dried, 108
  tomato-pesto bagel spread, sun-
    dried, 134
topping, creamy rum, 98
tortellini soup, quick, 185
Trail Mix, 71
treats, peanut butter krispy, 56
trout salad sandwich with dill
  dressing, smoked, 165
Tuna & Tartar Salad, 158-159

Vegetable Scramble, 139
vegetable
  lasagna, no more boil, 216-217
  matzo ball soup, quick less-fat,
    222-223
  spread, peanut butter, 54

weight loss, 5